THAT BLESSED LIBERTY:
EPISCOPAL BISHOPS AND THE DEVELOPMENT
OF THE AMERICAN REPUBLIC
1789-1860

Published in the United States of America by

Prolego Press
2721 Marine St.
South Bend, IN 46614

© Prolego Press 2025

ISBN: 978-1-7359230-8-6

Cover design: Ethan Greb

That Blessed Liberty:
Episcopal Bishops
and the
Development of the American Republic 1789-1860

Miles Smith IV and Adam Carrington

Foreword by Mark D. Tooley

PROLEGO PRESS

SOUTH BEND, INDIANA

Table of Contents

Foreword — vii

Introduction — xi

Part I: Visionaries
   William White — 1
   John Henry Hobart — 15
   George Washington Doane — 31

Part II: Missionaries
   Jackson Kemper — 47
   Philander Chase — 59
   James Hervey Otey — 71

Part III: Intellectuals
   John Stark Ravenscroft — 89
   Charles McIlvaine — 103
   John Henry Hopkins — 117
   William Meade — 131

Conclusion — 145

Acknowledgements — 153

Foreword

Early American religion is often mythologized as steadily Mainline Protestant or devoutly revivalist, sustaining a thoroughly Christian society before the advent of Twentieth Century secularism. The Protestant Episcopal Church, to which many of the Founders belonged, was, in this view, always the steady chaplain to America's elite.

Of course, the reality is far more complex and interesting. The United States's religious trajectory at its founding was far from certain. Anglicans in the early republic were significantly discredited by their ties to the Church of England. Some of its priests and many of its adherents had been Tories. Some had quit the colonies for the motherland. Could a church whose head had been Britain's king have utility in a rising republic defined by rebellion against that monarch?

The answer is gloriously yes, as illustrated by this story of ten key Protestant Episcopal Church bishops from the Founding until the Civil War. It was no easy task for America's early Anglicans to reorganize a new denomination fit for democracy while still affirming Anglican theology and ecclesiology, minus the role of Britain's monarch and parliament. Yet these ten bishops and their spiritual kindred amid turmoil and disagreement built a church that would never be very numerous but would always be very influential.

Their disagreements included the inevitable High Church versus Calvinist and evangelical perspectives always present in Anglican

DNA, compounded by the Oxford Movement's seductive call to Roman Catholicism or something just short. But these ten bishops were united in defining the Protestant Episcopal Church as firmly if widely Protestant. They also agreed about the church's support for the American democratic experiment, while carving out a privileged niche for their own denomination amid America's growing Protestant diversity.

After the American Revolution, the old religious state establishments were crumbling, while evangelical revivalism ascended, and Unitarianism attracted rationalist Christians like Thomas Jefferson and John Adams, who thought the Nicene Creed and the Trinity irrational. The Methodists, Baptists and Restorationists rejoiced at the overthrow of the Anglican and Congregationalist establishments. Their preachers and camp meetings populated the opening frontier. These ten bishops of the Protestant Episcopal Church, even amid their disputes, were certain that Anglican ecclesiology uniquely protected the Gospel from emotional excesses, anarchy, and apostasy.

Some of these ten bishops were reluctant to admit that other Protestant movements, especially the new revivalists, were even legitimately churches. Other bishops were more generous. But all agreed that the Protestant Episcopal Church uniquely and providentially could protect America from Roman Catholicism, impiety, and evangelical disorder. Bishop William White in Philadelphia literally ministered to the Founding Fathers who worshipped in his church. Bishop William Meade, born during George Washington's presidency, grieved his native Virginia's secession from the Union. The bishops in-between organized their new denomination, restored Anglicanism where it had retreated, and spread it to the frontier. They built colleges and seminaries, along with new gothic spires to replace the old brick and wood frame colonial structures, reflecting the Protestant Episcopal Church's emerging social ascendancy.

These ten bishops had an uneasy relationship with the Second Great Awakening that so deeply shaped the early republic during their lives and careers. That awakening largely replaced the old religious establishments in which Anglicanism had been central. But it also saved

America from the Unitarianism and more egregious forms of infidelity that many churchmen had feared. Republican America would not be republican France. It would be a mostly Christian republic with religious freedom for all. The Protestant Episcopal bishops carefully exploited the awakening to revive their old churches and plant new ones, while keeping the spiritually awakened tied to The Prayer Book.

Doing so often required fundraising in England, American Episcopal wealth not yet having accumulated to later Victorian levels. History has largely forgotten that these bishops and other early Protestant Episcopal clergy, no less than the Methodist circuit riders, had to endure hardships and travel thousands of miles on nearly impassable roads and roads and rivers to spread their message and build their new congregations. Long before country clubs where Episcopalians predominated, these bishops and others shared wagons or tavern rooms with frontier ruffians, requiring spiritual and physical courage. Early Protestant Episcopal clergy sometimes physically had to fight their way up the social ladder.

The ten bishops were united in their commitment to the American republic but uncertain about how to preserve its unity amid division over slavery. They were negative towards slavery and yet also averse to abolitionism. They mostly stayed away from direct political involvements, even as they mixed among America's most important leaders. Perhaps most importantly, these bishops and their ecclesial kindred led what became Mainline Protestantism into constructing America's wonderfully inclusive and ingenious civil religion. Protestant Episcopal churches and clergy, often as military or legislative chaplains, became the chief priestcraft for this civil religion. In often unconscious respect for Anglicanism's unique role in British civilization, the other Mainline Protestants typically yielded in these rites to their less numerous but more historically venerable berobed brethren.

This book about how the Protestant Episcopal Church and these ten bishops sustained American Christianity and shaped the republic is highly instructive for today's Episcopalians, Anglicans, Mainline Protestants, evangelicals, and others who seek steadier social models for public religion than what America typically experiences today. These ten bishops were not always correct in their views or actions. But the overall arc of their lives and careers as churchmen and as Americans is magnificent to behold.

Mark D. Tooley, July 2025

Introduction

In 1895 William S. Perry, Episcopal bishop of Iowa, published The Episcopate in America. It offered 400 or so biographical sketches of the bishops in the Protestant Episcopal Church, from its formation in 1789 to the Gilded Age. Perry told his readers "that the story of the introduction of the Anglican episcopate into America is full of incident. The lives of the men who have filled the office of bishop in the American Church are at once interesting and instructive." The contributions the bishops made "to American literature, even in the midst of absorbing labors and constant cares, are both creditable and important." By literature Perry meant literature, and the bishops of the Episcopal Church in the nineteenth century broadly proved to be men of letters, in culture, in politics, in religion, and in society. Perry's objective was "to tell the story of the struggle for the episcopate, to record briefly the lives of the bishops of the United States, and to furnish comprehensive lists of their literary works." He wanted to clothe a "dry skeleton of dates and facts... with such incidents and remarks as shall afford to the reader an understanding of their characters and the circumstances molding and influencing their lives." Although he was a churchman and a bishop, Perry wanted to write "in the spirit of historical impartiality. The effort has been made to supply the means for correctly estimating both the men and the measures marking their official careers."[1]

Perry wrote in an era where relatively few Americans attended Episcopal churches—only 720,000 Episcopal parishioners worshiped in 1900 when the national population was seventy-six million, compared to over 2.2 million Presbyterians—but the bishops exercised an outsized role in American civil religion and in influencing religious trends in the United States. The history of the Protestant Episcopal Church in the United States, many Episcopalians and quite a few non Episcopalians claimed, coincided with the history of the American republic and English settlement of North America. Samuel D. McConnell, an Episcopal minister in Philadelphia, wrote in 1890 that the Episcopal Church's life "is continuous from the beginning. It was first on the ground. It is of interest to all churchmen, and, for reasons I hope to make evident, ought to be to all Americans."[2]

The beginnings of the Episcopal church and an independent Anglican province for the North American republic were humble, and hardly a harbinger of the cultural and material success that defined the Episcopal Church at the beginning of the Twentieth Century. Massive Episcopal churches like St. John the Divine in New York City were unthinkable. Dioceses routinely had under 500 communicants, and Anglicanism was tainted by its association with the British crown. But that association did not last long. A concentrated effort by Episcopal bishops and laymen created a convincing and sustainable American Anglican churchmanship. Our story is that of the first generation of Episcopal bishops who put that new American Anglicanism to work between 1800 and the United States Civil War.

---

[1] William S. Perry, *The Episcopate in America: Sketches, Biographical and Bibliographical, of the American Church with a Preliminary Essay on the Historic Episcopate and Documentary Annals of the Introduction of the Anglican Line of Succession in to America* (New York: The Christian Literature Company, 1895), ix.

[2] Samuel D. McConnell, *History of the American Episcopal Church from the Planting of the Colonies to the End of the Civil War* (London: Sampson, Low, Marston, Searle, and Rivington, 1891), xiii.

INTRODUCTION

The formation of the Episcopal Church occurred in the aftermath of a conflict that gave rise to a particular type of Anglophobia. To justify the American Revolution, and especially the political act of independence, Britain, its king, and its church were increasingly identified by Patriot commentators as the source for all of America's woes. Thomas Jefferson's Declaration of Independence and Thomas Paine's *Common Sense* turned the quite pious George III into a tyrannical bogeyman who threatened to send bishops to serve as royal toadies and lord their unearned authority over free American (and now republican) citizens. When the first convention of the Episcopal Church met in its 1789 synod, it did so, Samuel Wilberforce later wrote, with "meekness and heavenly wisdom." Undoubtedly the perceptible meekness of the convention made a more enduring mark on the delegates and laymen and presbyters than any divine counsel. The convention's delegates numbered only a handful. The American Revolution decimated the institutional power of the Church of England, and only one state—South Carolina—retained any form of Anglican establishment by 1789. Wilberforce rightly noted that "the minds of men were still angry and unsettled. They knew little of the principles on which they were to act; and points of the utmost delicacy and moment were sure to come under consideration." The Constitution and American independence, however, were by 1789 an accomplished fact, and Anglican churchmen would have to work within the republican framework laid out in the laws of the United States if they wanted to heal their increasingly moribund church. The election of bishops was a priority, and so the gathered laymen and presbyters set to work carrying out in the new republic an ancient practice done by the apostles in the first century: electing bishops. "After setting forth their 'gratitude to God for having lately blessed the Protestant Episcopal Church in the United States of America with a complete and entire ministry,'" the convention declared "that to secure for their people 'the benefit and advantage of those offices, the administration of which belongs to the highest order of the ministry, and to encourage and promote a union of the whole Episcopal Church in their states, and to perfect and compact this mystical body of Christ, we do hereby nominate, elect, and appoint the Rev. Edward Bass, a presbyter of the Church, to be our bishop.'" Like the Anglican churchmen that preceded them for two centuries, these new American Anglicans upheld the time-honored practice of promising to render to their bishop "all canonical obedience and submission, when canonically consecrated and invested with the apostolic office and powers." This was not to be a democratic election done at the whims of laypeople. The "right reverend bishops in the states of Connecticut, New York, and Pennsylvania," heeded the prayers of the laity and consecrated their "said brother…canonically investing him with the apostolic office and powers."[3]

One of the first concerns the bishops addressed was how to pray for, and worship in, the new American republic. The prayer book was undoubtedly meant for a monarchy. Presidents had replaced kings; a republic replaced a kingdom. And so in the aftermath of the American Revolution, the newly Americanized Protestant Episcopal Church in the United States revised the Book of Common Prayer for American usage in 1785 and again in 1789. The reasons given were to make Anglican worship in the new American republic "conformable to the principles of the American Revolution and the constitutions of the several States." William White, the second American bishop and the first presiding bishop of the Episcopal Church, led the charge to Americanize Anglican liturgy. In his book *The American Prayer-Book Revisions of 1785 and 1789,* Bishop Perry of Iowa proposed that it was William White's patriotism that drove him to amend an Anglican liturgy largely unchanged since 1662. "It is certainly characteristic of the patriotic White," noted Perry, "as well as thoroughly consonant with the environment of the revisers of 1785, that this first American liturgical document should begin with words such as these: 'That in the suffrages,

---

[3] Carl H Esbeck and Jonathan J Den Hartog eds., *Disestablishment and Religious Dissent: Church–State Relations in the New American States, 1776–1833* (Columbia: University of Missouri Press, 2019), 181-202; Samuel Wilberforce, *A History of the Protestant Episcopal Church in America* (London: James Burns, 1844), 220-221.

after the Creed, instead of O Lord, save the King, be said, O Lord, bless and preserve these United States.'"[4]

Perry emphasized that pastoral concerns were symbiotic with patriotic expression in the preparations of the Prayer Book revisions in the 1780s. The laity, and lay political concerns, pushed churchmen to change the liturgy. Perry called the liturgical changes in the aftermath of the American victory in the War for Independence "a necessity." At the outbreak of the war, "clergy who continued to use the state prayers in the service were subjected to interruption and insult, and often to personal peril." As independence gained support and "took shape in the minds of the people, the clergy were forced to face the problem of ceasing their public ministrations, or of omitting these obnoxious prayers." In Philadelphia's Christ Church, "the first formal and authoritative change in the services took place, even before its chimes had sounded far and wide, ringing in response to the pealing of the State House bell – the proclamation of liberty to the world." When independence was declared on July 4, 1776, the vestry of Christ Church, "from among whose worshippers and pew-holders fully half a dozen of the 'signers' were furnished, met, and ordered the omission of the prayers for the king and royal family." The Prayer Book revisions illustrated how churchmen in the new Protestant Episcopal Church in the United States conceived of the relationship between the church and the political order. "The Churchmen of 1785," Bishop Perry declared, "were patriots." They shaped Episcopal services for the century that succeeded the American Revolution. Prayer Book revision was "done by the very men who, in the halls of congress or on the field of battle, won for us our independence." The American Book of Common Prayer after its revisions in 1785 and 1789 "was the first expression of the autonomy of the American Church thus breathing, to the God Who had given us our nationality, of the Church's prayer for the benediction and preservation of the United States!"[5]

[4] William Stevens Perry, *The American Prayer-book Revisions of 1785 and 1789: A Sermon Preached in Philadelphia, On the Eighteenth Sunday after Trinity, October 16, 1892* (Davenport, IA: Edward Borcherdt, 1892), 1-6.
[5] *Ibid.*

INTRODUCTION

The Americanization of the Episcopal Church remained a pastoral priority for the entirety of the antebellum era. In the Twenty-First Century, Anglican exoticism has been one of its chief appeals. But even High Churchmen of the Early Republic like John Henry Hobart rebuked the tendency of Americans to idealize the Old World or exotic forms of tradition, and he had no time for cultural or ecclesiastical anti-American traditionalism that rejected the constitutional settlement. As late as the fall of 1825, he preached a sermon addressing the relationship of the United States to other countries, particularly Great Britain. The 1820s saw the publication of travelogues from American literary luminaries, such as Washington Irving, James Fenimore Cooper, and others which stoked a mania for European travel and forms of socio-political exoticism. Hobart saw celebration of Europe as problematic, and he went so far as to address the necessity of patriotic affection for the American republic from the pulpit. The bishop understood parishioners had "perhaps sighed for those distant climes, whose skies are represented as glowing with serene and almost perpetual radiance, and whose breezes bear health and cheeriness to the decaying and languid frame." He admitted that "in these respects, it would be little less than absurd to urge a superiority over some other lands, or altogether an equality with them." Natural beauty in the Old World routinely drew American travelers and American exultation. The Alps, the Italian villas of old, and the great romantic landscapes of Europe certainly impressed even the most patriotic Americans, but Hobart refused to concede that the United States was not as beautiful as Europe, and whatever beauty existed in Europe carried with it the weight of eons of ecclesiastical and political oppression. "We boast not indeed of Alps rising on Alps with wild and snow-crowned summits, sheltering within their precipitous and lofty ridges, valleys that beam with the liveliest verdure, and bear the richest productions of the earth." But even "the warmest admirer of nature, after having feasted on these tremendously sublime or exquisitely beautiful scenes," still turned "with refreshing pleasure to the contemplation of the varied and bold outlines that mark the extensive mountains which range through our own country." Travelers in the

United States observed "highly cultivated fields that occupy their valleys and variegate the massy forests which mount up their sides." Great rovers proudly traversed the plains, "or burst through the lofty hills which oppose them." Skies, "if not always as genial," were "often as serene and glowing as that of the most favoured of the southern regions of Europe, and which illumines the fertile soil that it nourishes and enriches."[6]

Hobart's delight in Europe was limited. He tempered his glorification of the moral legacy of the Old World with a patriotic exclamation of American superiority from the pulpit. It was, declared the bishop, the United States' "civil and religious institutions that we may, without the imputation of vainglory, boast the preeminence." Actual observation, he asserted, compelled "every traveler through those nations of the continent that now submissively yield to the yoke of despotic power mild and benevolent as in some instances is its administration," to understand, "however reluctant, the full force of the remark, which he may have thought evil discontent alone had raised, that the labour and independence and freedom and happiness of the many are sacrificed to the ambition and power and luxury of the few." Hobart and his fellow bishops understood their mission to be the formation of a Protestant Episcopal Church for the American republic, and not an escapist religious traditionalism.[7]

Theologically, the Episcopal Church fit in the broad mainstream of American Protestant thought in the Nineteenth Century. Debates over the Calvinism in the Church, for example, were not synonymous with debates over whether the Episcopal Church stood downstream from the theology of the Sixteenth Century Reformation. In 1820 William White, Episcopal bishop of Pennsylvania, published *Memoirs of the Protestant Episcopal Church in the United States of America*. The work catalogued and narrated the history of the Episcopal Church from its

---

[6] John Henry Hobart, *The United States of America Compared with Some European Countries, Particularly England: In a Discourse Delivered in Trinity Church, and in St. Paul's and St. John's Chapels, in the City of New York, October, 1825* (New York: T. and J. Swords, 1826), 8-11
[7] Ibid.

xvii

advent in 1789. White enlarged the work in a second edition published in 1836. Episcopalians remained substantively unified theologically until the 1840s, when the Tractarian controversy occurred. That unity lay in an understanding that the Thirty-Nine Articles of the Church of England were Reformed. The disagreements that did occur among presbyters and lay intellectuals was not over whether the Episcopal Church was Reformed or not, but how the term Reformed was defined. All but the most vocal Calvinists in the Episcopal Church rejected the association of Anglicanism with the Westminster Confession and Presbyterianism, but Episcopalians nonetheless regularly appealed to Sixteenth Century Reformed thinkers like John Calvin, Martin Bucer, and Heinrich Bullinger. At the Episcopal Church's 1801 convention a debate over the place of the Articles occurred between Calvinists and those who refused to self-describe as Calvinist. The debate was not, as it might seem to modern readers, a question of whether or not the Episcopal Church was a Protestant or even Reformed church.[8]

Bishop White argued that the Church of England's theological dispositions remained Reformed and he put the Articles of Religion in the category of a Reformed confession. What the bishops particularly questioned was whether or not the Articles should be amended to clarify their theological commitments in light of the Arminian controversy that had been resurrected by the rise of Methodism in Britain in the Eighteenth Century. Calvinism, the Bishop noted, "came in greater authority from Geneva" during the reign of Elizabeth I. The "constant complaint" about the Articles from the Puritans, White proposed, lay not in the fact that the Articles weren't Reformed, but that they were not "sufficiently evangelical" in the matter of particular commitments regarding the controversy between Calvinists and the followers of Jacobus Arminius. The Puritans' mistake, said White, was not their commitments to Calvinism but in asking the Articles to do something they were not designed to do: speak to a controversy that began a generation

---

[8] William White, *Memoirs of the Protestant Episcopal Church in the United States of America From its Organization to the Present Day* (New York: Swords, Standford and Co., 1836), 186-187.

after they were written and promulgated. "It may be proved," the bishop noted, "that in the reign of Edward VI when the articles were framed, there was a diversity of sentiments" within Reformed churches on what he called "those points," particularly certain questions over the limits of atonement and the nature of perseverance. White proposed that at the time of the Elizabethan settlement none of the disputants committed to various positions within broader Reformed churches "complained" that narrow theological pronouncements on the controversial issues had been excluded. The Church of England's mission had been to create a Reformed Catholic church, and had seen fit to not exclude certain positions. The Articles defined Reformed religiosity for the Church of England and later the Episcopal Church, but they were older than Westminster and did not speak to the same controversies, nor did they speak as narrowly on certain controversies within Reformed Protestantism. "It is but to compare the Thirty-Nine Articles with the Westminster confession, or with the decrees of the synod of Dort," White wrote, "to perceive how general and guarded the first were, on the topics on which the others are very particular and express." The bishops decided not to amend the articles. "A new code of articles" would split "the Church into no one knows how many different communions, very much to the hindrance of true piety." White supposed that the explicitly Reformed Articles still approached "nearer than others, to the standard of the best ages." Debates over the Articles and Calvinism before the Tractarian controversy were not ever debates over the Protestant or Reformed nature of the Episcopal Church and its predecessors, but debates over theological controversies within Reformed Protestantism.[9]

Episcopal bishops in the nineteenth century cared deeply about the health of the American republic and its peoples. Their most prominent ventures in culture, education, and politics gained them accolades, but fundamentally they remained pastors whose chief interest was their local flocks. Like all Protestants in the era, the catechesis of children and family worship remained a vital part of Episcopal life in the Early

[9] *Ibid.*

Republic. Northern bishops like Jonathan Mayhew Wainwright and southerners like John Stark Ravenscroft highlighted the importance of the daily offices and family worship. Families in particular formed what Ravenscroft believed was the most important part of Christian ministry, and he particularly worried about what he saw was laxity towards family worship in his diocese. "The observance and cultivation of family religion," he argued, increased and advanced "true godliness" in society at large. Without the "root and spring, under God, of 'all holy desires, all good counsels, and all just works,' hope is vain for the Church and the state; we shall sink into a nation of infidels." Family religion in the Episcopal context of the Early Republic generally denoted the reading of shorter forms of Morning and Evening prayer by the head of the household. Ravenscroft tied family worship explicitly to the health of the church and the state. The decline in the practice harmed the families of devout Christians and their secular neighbors. "That the practice has declined in the families of professing Christians; that it is abandoned in all others, is known by all who hear me at this moment." Ravenscroft lamented the fact that non-believers—or the non-devout—historically might have participated in some form of Christian devotion but no longer did. Even non-church-attending citizens, the bishop hoped, understood that Christian practice was a societal good, whether they were spiritually committed to Christianity or not. The consequences of the decline in family worship, the bishop declared, "are the bitter fruit of increasing crime and profaneness" which were "recorded in every court, and witnessed by every Sabbath." [10]

Ravenscroft attached the moral denigration recorded in courthouses and on the sabbath—civil and religious decay—to the failure of the Christian family. Ultimately, the future of the civil, social, and spiritual health of the American republic rested on Christian families, according to Ravenscroft. Would the United States' potential decay be so, "were the principles of our holy religion early and carefully instilled

---

[10] John Stark Ravenscroft, *The Works of the Right Reverend John Stark Ravenscroft* Vol. I (New York: Protestant Episcopal Press, 1830), 111-112.

into the minds of the rising hope of this great and growing Christian nation?" If the fear of God, and the reverence of his most holy name, and the observance of his worship, and the knowledge of his life-giving precepts were "inculcated and manifested in our families," the result would be seen throughout the world. "Awake, then, from this torpor, ye Christian fathers and mothers!!" North Carolina's prelate thundered that Christians must awaken from "this deadly delusion of adulterated religion, which is so fast swallowing up the dearest hope you can entertain of a happy eternity, with those who are dearest to you here." Christian fathers and mothers as well as right religious practice for families, Ravenscroft proposed, held the key to the civil, social, and spiritual health of Americans and the American republic.[11]

The numerical apotheosis and then decline of the mainline and ecclesiastical fracture of the last sixty years has left Anglicanism in North America truncated in a way unthinkable, a consequence of which was diminished ecclesiastical and theological memory of every major Anglican body in North America. It is unlikely that parishioners in the Episcopal Church or ACNA know the history of the formation of the Episcopal church or the history of the growth of Anglican churchmanship in the United States. This work is not a comprehensive history of the formation of the Protestant Episcopal Church in the Early Republic United States, nor is it an encyclopedic record of the lives of the Church's prelates. Instead, it is meant to provide helpful biographical vignettes of churchmen who exercised noteworthy influence on culture, politics, religion, and society in the United States between the founding of the American republic at the end of the Eighteenth century, and the Civil War. In many ways the era between the American Revolution and the Civil War saw stability and unity in the Episcopal Church. The initial generation of Episcopal prelates were shaping the church in an era before the rise of en masse nationalist civil religion, mass popular culture, and debates over Darwinism clouded theological discussion in the Gilded Age, and therefore were generally less influenced by the

[11] *Ibid.*

ideology of nationalist Protestantism that created the debates that led to the Fundamentalist/Modernist Controversy at the beginning of the Twentieth Century. While there has never been an era of absolute unity within the Episcopal Church or North American Anglicanism broadly, the first half of the Nineteenth Century saw meaningful cooperation between High Churchmen and evangelicals to perpetuate a unified conception of Anglican churchmanship in the young American republic. Even early Tractarian sympathizers in the 1830s and 1840s would be unrecognizable to modern Anglo-Catholics, who claim to be the successors of nineteenth century High Churchmen. Bishops like John Henry Hopkins and James Hervey Otey, both convinced High Churchmen who voiced vocal sympathy with the Tractarian movement, regularly disciplined and rebuked presbyters in their diocese for the use of altar candles, the display of crucifixes, and other liturgical and vestmental practices that are now ubiquitous in all types of Anglican Churches.

Understanding the era of initial Anglican formation in the United States is vital to the perpetuation of Anglicanism. In the aftermath of the Episcopal church's ecclesiastical and theological decline and the rise of highly syncretic so-called Evangelical religion, Anglicanism is often defined merely by its liturgy and its ostensible lack of a theological identity. In fact, the Protestant Episcopal Church in the Early Republic had a definable, enforceable, and sustainable theological identity that the bishops carefully preserved, even as they maintained a wide latitude of practice in the province. Evangelical, Old High Churchman, and Tractarian undeniably had their squabbles, but the fundamentally Protestant and Anglican nature of the Protestant Episcopal Church was never denied. Anglicanism was not, as it's increasingly come to be in the Twenty-First Century, an absence of a theological identity, nor did the bishops believe their liturgy was an acceptable substitute for theology.

Part I

Visionaries

William White
1748-1836

Patriarch of the American Episcopal Church.[1] This unofficial title was conferred on William White both in his own time and by later biographers. More than any other churchman, White helped to form the Protestant Episcopal Church as an institution. He articulated grounds for its organization in the American Revolution's aftermath that accounted for its break with the Church of England and the increasing democratization and egalitarianism of the newly independent United States. He then played an important part in implementing many of these structures and concepts, both in the years immediately after the Revolution and into the country's Early Republic era. White also was the first American bishop consecrated by the Church of England, going on to participate in the consecration of every American Episcopal bishop from 1792 through 1836. During his bishopric, White served as rector of important parishes in Philadelphia. Moreover, he wrote extensively on the Protestant Episcopal Church's beliefs and organization. In these works and in his actions, White shepherded the young Church toward a relatively broad catholicity that refused to fall squarely within one particular ecclesiastical camp. He imprinted his DNA onto the church in ways that continue to this day in both The

---

[1] Julia Hammond Ward, *The Life and Times of Bishop White* (New York: Dodd Mead and Company, 1892), 11.

PART I: VISIONARIES

Episcopal Church (TEC) and the Anglican Church in North America (ACNA).

William's father was Thomas White. Thomas was born in London in 1704 but sailed to Maryland at age sixteen.[2] His mother was a woman by the maiden name of Esther Hewlings. Esther's family had been Quakers but joined the Church of England while living in Burlington, New Jersey. When the two married in Philadelphia, it was the second marriage for each as both Thomas and Esther's first spouses had passed away. William White was born to the couple on April 4, 1748 in the city of Philadelphia.[3] A year later, his sister Mary was born. She one day would marry Robert Morris—a signer of the Declaration of Independence, the Articles of Confederation, the Constitution, and the man who served as Superintendent of Finance of the United States from 1781-1784.[4]

White received baptism as an infant and was raised in a Philadelphia parish. That city would remain the center of White's personal and ministerial endeavors for the rest of his life. The future bishop took an early interest in religious matters, giving special credit to his mother's Christian instruction during his childhood. A childhood friend recounted how White from a very early age would play "church," acting as the minister and giving a sermon to his companions, usually on the topic of being good.[5]

At age 17, White graduated from the College of Philadelphia (later the University of Pennsylvania) of which his father had been a founding trustee.[6] During this time, White and four other students interested in ministry gave a series of lectures on Sunday evenings about,

---

[2] Bird Wilson, *Memoir of the Life of the Right Reverend William White* (Philadelphia: James Kay, Jun. and Brother, 1839), 12-13.
[3] John Nichols Norton, *The Life of the Rt. Rev. William White* (New York: General Protestant Episcopal S. School Union and Church Book Society, 1856), 10.
[4] Ward, 13.
[5] Wilson, *Memoir*, 21.
[6] William Stevens Perry, *The History of the American Episcopal Church, 1587-1883* (Boston: James R. Good & Co., 1885), 2: 459; Wilson, 16.

"the history of the Bible."[7] White recounted that conducting these sessions equipped the men with a wide-ranging knowledge of theological topics and extensive practice in public speaking. This training would bear much fruit for White's future ministry.

Though he wished to enter Holy Orders, White ran into geographical troubles. The colonies had no localized bishop. Instead, the entire region resided under the care of the Bishop of London. After mastering his theological studies, White sailed to England in 1770 to receive ordination to the diaconate from Richard Terrick, then London's bishop. After his December 23rd ordination, he remained in London until he reached the age at which he could join the priesthood. This ordination took place in June of 1772.[8] Soon after his return to the States, White became assistant minister of St. Peter's and Christ Church, two Philadelphia parishes served by one set of clergy.

On February 11th of the following year, White married Mary Harrison. It was a powerful match. Her father had been a successful merchant and then, in the 1760s, mayor of Philadelphia. Mary would bear William eight children, though, sadly, only three would live past childhood.[9]

Two years later, the Revolutionary War began. While many Church of England clergy in the colonies sided with the Mother country, White aligned early with the struggle for Independence. During the conflict, White served as a chaplain to the Continental Congress, a post he retained in most years through the war, with the Articles of Confederation Congress, and into the Constitutional era, finally leaving the post for good in 1801.[10] He would be a consistent defender of the Revolution throughout his public life, giving and eventually publishing a sermon on Romans 13 that interpreted the American Revolution as

---

[7] Ward, 20.
[8] Norton, 21.
[9] Episcopal General Convention, *Archives of the General Convention, Volume 1: The Correspondence of John Henry Hobart*, edited by Arthur Lowndes (New York: 1911), 344.
[10] Norton, 27, 29.

consistent with its commands.[11] White's support for the Revolution also partook of a broader public participation in the country's political life. Unlike his friend, Bishop John Henry Hobart, Bishop White participated in political affairs in several ways during his ministry. He helped form the American Colonization Society, which infamously sought to relocate African-Americans from America to Africa. Moreover, White lent public support to those backing Greece's revolt against the Turks in 1823 and later asked that the national government keep its pledges to the Cherokee tribe. He gave a sermon detailing his views of the relationship between church and state at a service for a day of public thanksgiving proclaimed by President George Washington in 1795. There, he argued for the close relationship between government and religion with links between their duties and mutual but free support between their institutions.[12] President George Washington was a regular attender at the services he officiated, and White served as chaplain at a Congressionally-established oration commemorating the life of the president upon that great man's death.

Returning to the Revolutionary period, White rose to national prominence toward that war's end, mostly through the publication in 1782 of *The Case of the Episcopal Church in the United States Considered*.[13] In it, he articulated principles of organization for the American Church in the Revolution's aftermath. In general, many thought the Church of England too tied to monarchy to work in a polity, like America's, that was based on popular government. Yet White made the case for his Church's conformity with American political principles. He admitted differences. In particular, the Church no longer could submit to the spiritual jurisdiction of the Church of England, because, "such a [foreign] dependence is contrary to the fundamental principles of civil society, and therefore

---

[11]   William White, *A Sermon the Duty of Obedience as Required in Scripture* (Philadelphia: John Ormrod, 1799).

[12]   White, *A Sermon on the Reciprocal Influence of Civil Policy and Religious Duty* (Philadelphia: Ormrod and Comrad, 1795).

[13]   Sidney A. Temple, *The Commonsense Theology of Bishop White* (New York: King's Crown Press, 1846), 21-22.

cannot be required by the Scriptures."[14] White also stressed that the new American Church could not hold the same relationship to the state as did the English Church. In England, the Church was regulated by the Convocation of the clergy and the convened Parliament together. Parliament's role formed part of the Church of England's status as the state established Church. Parliament also formed the means for lay participation in Church government to go along with the clergy's governing role. However, instead of state establishments, White noted that the American Church's "future continuance can be provided for only by voluntary associations for union and good government."[15]

Still, White wished to modify these forms in what would become the Protestant Episcopal Church, not to remake them entirely. For one, he sought to translate the Mother church's joint rule of clergy and laity to the American context in some form. Doing so, he believed, could be a reasonable amendment of episcopal government also consistent with the new country's political and social principles. Thus, he believed that, "[t]he power of electing a superior order of ministers, ought to be in the clergy and laity together."[16] He also argued for the American church to understand parishes not as subdivisions of dioceses, as was the case in England, but as the foundation for the organization of larger collectives. These parishes, moreover, would be fundamentally equal to each other, not subject to the diocesan cathedral as was the case in England. In relation to this restructuring, White sketched in outline ideas for a General Convention to be held every three years.[17] He also suggested a minimal standard for ministerial doctrinal subscription, to, "extend no farther than an acknowledgment of the Scriptures as a rule of faith and life," though he immediately added that "some general sanction may be given to the thirty-nine articles of religion, so as to adopt their leading sense."[18] Yet this point, too, was qualified. The

---

[14] White, *The Case of the Episcopal Churches in the United States Considered* (Philadelphia: David C. Claypool, 1782), 6.
[15] Ibid., 7.
[16] White, *The Case of the Episcopal Church*, 8.
[17] Ibid., 10-11.
[18] Ibid., 11.

general sanction must consist of "a chain of union," not "exacting entire uniformity of sentiment," for which he claimed the Articles inadequate.[19] Worship, moreover, should continue according to a Prayer Book modified but only "moderately" so as to make it conform to the new circumstances of American independence. Finally, church discipline in the form of excommunication should be possible in theory but passingly rare in application.

Moreover, White wrote that the American church remained committed to the episcopal form of government and rejected claims that such a system only could exist in a political monarchy, not a republic. The American Episcopal Church, then, should seek its own bishops in line with Apostolic succession. However, where and while doing so proved impossible, he denied that either bishops or succession was essential for the church's continuation.[20] White argued that "the worship of God and the instruction and reformation of the people are the principal objects of ecclesiastical discipline; if so, to relinquish them from a scrupulous adherence to Episcopacy is sacrificing the substance to the ceremony."[21] A temporary deviation from this form of government was warranted when the other option was the withering of the Church while it waited for an episcopal vine. Among other sources, White looked to the Formularies for support. Article 36 merely declared the order of bishops, priests, and deacons "not repugnant to the word of God," which White read as an endorsement of its rightness but not its essentialness.[22] The American Episcopal Church's situation resembled what happened when Queen Elizabeth took the throne after her half-sister, "Bloody Mary," where non-episcopal ordinations for Protestant refugees to the continent were accepted.

This essay later received criticism and dismissal by the High Church party within the Protestant Episcopal Church, particularly on the importance of the episcopal form of government. Some argued that

[19] Ibid.
[20] Temple, 25-27.
[21] White, *Case of Episcopal Churches*, 16.
[22] Ibid., 17-18.

White himself never fully believed these arguments and later fully repudiated them. However, this argument does not hold water.[23] As we will discuss, he would reiterate the substance of his views on the episcopacy well into his episcopacy and saw that position as part of the DNA of the Protestant Episcopal Church.

Great Britain formally recognized American independence the following year, 1783, in the Treaty of Paris. How to address the ecclesiastical problems attending this political outcome then came to a head. In 1784, Samuel Seabury received ordination as the first American bishop. However, he was consecrated by bishops within the Scottish Episcopal Church, not the Church of England. Upon returning to the States the next year, Seabury organized a diocese in his home state of Connecticut. But Connecticut remained set apart from the episcopal parishes in most of the rest of the new country with lingering questions regarding the status of Seabury's consecration.

The same year—1785—the states of New York, New Jersey, Delaware, Pennsylvania, Maryland, Virginia, and South Carolina sent delegates for a convention held at Christ Church in Philadelphia over which White served as president.[24] The convention adopted a constitution, revised the 1662 Prayer Book, and wrote up an appeal to the English Church asking it to consecrate bishops for the church in the States. The Prayer Book revision passed the convention, with White's approval, but failed to gain broader assent. Part of its failure came from the fact that it made more than moderate adjustments to the Prayer Book. It dropped the Nicene and Athanasian creeds, made extensive cuts to the Thirty-Nine Articles, and required liturgical observance of July 4th, among many other revisions.[25] The later, approved 1789 edition would pull back from many (though not all) of these proposals.

---

[23] William Stevens Perry, *The History*, 2:9.
[24] E. Clowes Chorley, "The General Conventions of 1785, 1786, and 1789" in *Historical Magazine of the Protestant Episcopal Church* 4(4)(December 1935): 252.
[25] *Ibid.*, 254-255.

These attempts at reform were part of a commitment by White also seen in his 1782 essay. White sought to form the Protestant Episcopal Church on broad, more latitudinarian ground regarding matters of faith and practice. Here, White was deeply influenced by the thought of John Locke, including the English thinker's philosophical, political, and theological writings.[26] Not just in 1782 but throughout his ministry, he respected and argued from the Church of England's Formularies but did not wish for strict subscription to the Thirty-Nine Articles. Moreover, he called the Prayer Book a "venerable enclosure of our orthodoxy"[27] while approving significant changes for it largely on the basis of broadening who could adhere to it.

This broadness, though, certainly had limits. For one, it was decidedly Protestant. He declared Scripture "our principle instruction" in matters of faith and practice. He also rejected transubstantiation,[28] was critical of Roman Catholic views regarding the use of images,[29] and decisively rejected the Pope's claims over the universal church.[30] At the same time, White enforced certain particulars within Protestantism. He affirmed the Scriptural, ancient, and practical supports for the Episcopacy even if he did not declare churches unable to obtain it illegitimate. For another, White also argued against a Calvinist reading of Scripture, Church history, and the Formularies, writing an extensive work on the topic.[31] In his discussion of the Church Fathers, he located the introduction of Calvinistic readings of predestination to the Fourth Century, saying Chrysostom among others wrongly made the doctrine one about God's knowledge of individuals' salvation. He even criticized Augustine

---

[26] Temple, 12, 47.
[27] William White, *Bishop White's Opinions on Certain Theological and Ecclesiastical Points* (New York: Henry Onderdonk & Company, 1846), 105. Though White did endorse the Thirty-Nine Articles as "better than any other" rule, "likely to be obtained under present circumstances." See White, Memoirs of the Protestant Episcopal Church, 165.
[28] White, *Lectures*, 127-136.
[29] Ibid., 313-332.
[30] Ibid., 404-424.
[31] William White, *Comparative Views of the Controversy Between the Calvinists and the Arminians* (Philadelphia: M. Thomas, 1817).

on this score, arguing that he fell into error in his response to the Pelagians by taking the next step to say God not only knows but ordains who will be saved. In relation to these views, he at one point stated a hesitancy on the part of the Protestant Episcopal Church to adopt the Thirty-Nine Articles in the American Prayer Book due to the number of English Churchmen who read the formulary in a Calvinistic sense.[32]

After the meeting in 1785, the first truly General Convention took place the next year, in 1786. There, the Convention sought to choose candidates for the office of bishop, since the English Church now had agreed to consecrate. White (from Pennsylvania), Samuel Provoost (from New York), and David Griffith (from Virginia) were selected. Griffith declined while, in November of 1786, White and Provoost set sail for England. They both were consecrated on February 4th, 1787, in Lambeth Chapel.[33] With Seabury, the Protestant Episcopal Church now had three bishops. Within two years, the Connecticut diocese formally joined the other dioceses at a General Convention held in 1789.[34] The American Episcopal Church now was one. To ensure no controversy, the American church did not install any of its own bishops until a third had been consecrated in England. That happened in 1790, when James Madison, cousin to the more famous Founder, also was consecrated. From that point, future consecrations of bishops took place in America by American bishops, with Thomas John Claggett (of Maryland) being the first in 1792.

White was without doubt the most influential and consequential of this original set of American bishops.[35] He served from 1795 till his death as Presiding Bishop, since the position then went to the longest-serving bishop at the time. This role for him involved more than a plumb for seniority. He used his abilities locally, regionally, and nationally to build the Protestant Episcopal Church into a formidable ecclesiastical body within the United States. First, he expanded the number

---

[32] White, *Opinions*, 132.
[33] Norton, 38.
[34] *Ibid.*, 40.
[35] Perry, 2: 468.

PART I: VISIONARIES

of its ministers. As noted before, from 1795 until 1836, White officiated at the consecration of every new bishop in the United States—26 total. These included bishops across the spectrum of belief and practice within the Protestant Episcopal Church. However, among his proudest consecrations was that of John Henry Hobart to the Bishop's seat of New York—White having baptized and confirmed Hobart as well.[36] Hobart would become the pillar of the High Church party within the Protestant Episcopal Church. The two men remained close until Hobart's death in 1830, even if White did not share all of Hobart's High Church views.

Second, White built up his own parishes. While serving as a bishop, he also cared for two congregations in Philadelphia—St. Peter's and Christ Church—serving as rector at them for a total of 57 years. This care included many spiritual, political, and physical challenges. High among them was an onslaught of yellow fever that gripped Philadelphia in 1793. While removing his family to greater safety, White remained in the city to minister to the sick and the dying at great personal risk.[37] White's successful ministry throughout these years caused such growth in the Philadelphia area that another parish was needed to accommodate the influx of parishioners. In 1809, a new church building, named St. James, was consecrated in Philadelphia.[38] Bishop White served as its rector in addition to his care for Christ Church and St. Peter's. The growth did not end there. During his bishopric, White would see eight more churches added within the city.

At the same time that the Protestant Episcopal Church flourished in the City of Brotherly Love, it grew at a much slower pace throughout the rest of the Diocese. The "Society for the Advancement of Christianity in Pennsylvania" was formed in 1812 to address this problem. By the end of White's ministry, it had born significant fruit in the

---

[36] Ward, 109-110.
[37] Wilson, 158.
[38] *Ibid.*, 200; Norton, 60.

rest of the state—at his death, the number of parishes in his diocese had grown to 91.[39]

Third, White participated in the formation of theological education for both ministers and lay persons. Based on his own teaching, he wrote works on ordination,[40] a history of the Protestant Episcopal Church,[41] and a commentary on its catechism.[42] During his bishopric, White also saw the establishment of several seminaries for training clergy. This included the establishment of the General Theological Seminary in New York, a project agreed to at the General Convention in 1814. Additional institutions were established in Ohio (Kenyon) and Virginia (Virginia Theological Seminary) during this period as well.

White's time as a bishop involved much vocational triumph. But he also faced trials. These trials included significant personal tragedy. The year 1797 stood out on this score. First, White lost his thirteen-year old son William, who others recalled as exhibiting many of his father's virtues. Second, White later in the year faced the death of his wife, Mary.[43] Though a deep personal sting and a daunting spiritual trial, White continued serving his parishes, diocese, and the greater Protestant Episcopal Church throughout.

In his vocation, White also faced challenges. Significant among them, he saw divisions manifest within the Protestant Episcopal Church between its so-called "High Church" and "Low Church" or "Evangelical" factions. White sought to keep these divisions from causing too much discord within the church as the debates between the sides could be rancorous. White did so in pursuit of peace and unity, a posture consistent with his inclusive perspective. Also, in line with these views, it is difficult to place White squarely within either party. He defended a view

---

[39] Norton, 63.
[40] William White, *Commentaries Suited to the Occasion of Ordination* (New York: Swords, Stanford, and Co., 1833).
[41] White, *Memoirs of the Protestant Episcopal Church in the United States* (Philadelphia: S. Potter and Co., 1820). Another edition with additions by White came out in 1836.
[42] White, *Lectures on the Catechism of the Protestant Episcopal Church* (Philadelphia: Bradford and Innskeep, 1813).
[43] Norton, 53.

of baptismal regeneration in line with the High Churchmen of his day. On this point, he argued for an immediate, automatic baptismal regeneration of infants, saying that "this ordinance" is "an actual grafting into the Church, without any such distinction as the one invented between a visible and an invisible society under that name."[44] Scripture supported this view of baptismal regeneration, White declared, and the Formularies' language was clear on that score, too. In this view, he sided with the High Church party.

At the same time, he wrote an entire essay, finished in 1819, that critiqued the High Church party's view of the episcopacy.[45] In that work, consistent with his earlier *The Case of the Episcopal Church*, he argued against the idea "that to the being of a church Episcopacy is essential." He reiterated that he found no such principle in any decisions made by the Church of England. Such a view even contradicted the Ordinal and Article 19 of the Articles of Religion, both of which defined the true church in a way that omitted the episcopacy's necessity for ordination and legitimate sacraments. In the Prayer Book's prayer for all conditions of men, moreover, we petition for, "all who profess and call themselves Christians," with the assumption that such professing Christians "are of the said body."[46] Contrary thinking, White argued, critically delegitimized the Protestant Reformation and paved the way for theological movement toward Rome. However, he cautioned strongly against going to the other extreme about Bishops as well, arguing for a, "safe & Protestant Ground, on which to rest the Point of Episcopacy." This sure Reformational ground consisted of Scripture as "[t]he standard of divine truth." However, even in his doctrine of Scripture, he sought some kind of moderation. Holding up the Scriptures as the ultimate authority, he elsewhere added that, "next to them, the writings of those who were

[44] White, *Bishop White's Opinions*, 89.
[45] See William White, "An Essay on High-Church Principles" reproduced in full in Cynthia McFarland, "Bishop William White's 'An Essay on High-Church Principles'" in Anglican and Episcopal History 70(1)(March 2001): 4-39.
[46] White makes a similar argument in reference to the prayer for the church militant.

nearest to the times of the Apostles" should be consulted.[47] He then critiqued those Protestants who ignored or denigrated the Church Fathers as if doing so was necessary to affirm the primacy of God's Word.

Time eventually took its toll on the bishop. Though robust for his age, the duties of so large a diocese and regarding nationwide church matters eventually became too much. In 1827, when Bishop White was approaching 80 years old, Henry Onderdonk was consecrated as Assistant Bishop. He took over the visitation and oversight of distant parishes, while Bishop White focused on the area in and near Philadelphia.[48] Active till the end, White officiated for the last time at St. Peter's on June 26, 1836. He died a few weeks later on July 17th. He was 88 years old.

One cannot rightly conceive of the Protestant Episcopal Church without William White. He was and is a giant in its formation and in its continued identity. Partly through White's efforts, the Protestant Episcopal Church became comfortably established within American society, growing in numbers and influence. As he did so much at the start, so the Anglican tradition in the United States continues to bear various marks of White's vision up to this day.

On Sunday, July 24, Bishop George Washington Doane preached a eulogy sermon for the deceased White. He chose as his Scripture text Proverbs 4:18—"But the path of the just is as the shining light, that shineth more and more unto the perfect day." In his effusive eulogy, Doane called White,

> The excellent citizen, the amiable neighbour, the kind and generous friend, the faithful preacher of the Gospel, the Bishop, who, for fifty years, has fed the flock of God, —the Patriarch, revered, beloved and honoured of our family in Christ -the link that, through the Bishops of

---

[47] White, *Bishop White's Opinions*, 30-31.
[48] *Ibid.*, 75.

PART I: VISIONARIES

Christ's Church, knits us with ancient Saints and holy Martyrs, and Apostles, and the Lord himself.[49]

White rejected the claim by King James I of, "no bishop, no king, and no king, no bishop."[50] But so great was his footprint, that we might say that, no Bishop White, then no Protestant Episcopal Church as we have then and now know it.

---

[49] George Washington Doane, *The Path of the Just: A Sermon in Commemoration of the Right Reverend William White* (Burlington: J.L. Powell Missionary Press, 1836), 29.

[50] White, *The Case of the Episcopal Churches*, 16.

John Henry Hobart
1775-1830

Some consider the hardest struggles of the Episcopal Church to have taken place in the Twenty-first Century. These difficulties include membership decline, doctrinal drift, and structural division.

Though of a different nature, the Episcopal Church has faced other severe challenges in its American past. After the American Revolution, the remains of the Church of England were in a terrible state. During the Colonial period, the parishes had suffered the effects of neglect, with no bishop of their own and sparse attention paid to them by the Bishop of London, under whose care they superficially were. Many clergymen then had sided with Great Britain in the war, sowing doubts regarding the American Church's loyalty in the newly-founded American republic. In many parts of the country, parishes were few. Those that existed were under-served by inadequate clergy and generally faced either an indifferent or outright antagonistic society.

It was in this state of the Episcopal Church that John Henry Hobart served. Along with other bishops who arose at this time, Bishop Hobart helped revitalize the Protestant Episcopal Church in America. He served the Diocese of New York as its assisting, then diocesan bishop from 1811 to 1830. He took a diocese weak in piety, in clergy, and in number of parishioners, and grew it into a major force. Beyond the New York diocese, Hobart also would take his place as the leader of the High Church party across the entire Protestant Episcopal Church.

PART I: VISIONARIES

Hobart was born in the city of Philadelphia on September 14th, 1775.[1] His father passed away when he was one year old. Though raised without his father, Hobart received attentive care from his mother, herself a pious woman. In God's providence, Hobart was baptized by William White, then presbyter and later bishop of Pennsylvania. The same man also confirmed Hobart, ordained him to the diaconate and priesthood, as well as participated in his consecration as bishop.[2] Though White would attempt to stay above the party disputes of the Protestant Episcopal Church of the time, he considered the more partisan, High Church Hobart a close friend and generally a co-belligerent in churchly matters.

As a young man, Hobart was reputed as one adept at and interested in the business world. His biographers note that he could have pursued a more worldly calling in that sphere with great success. However, after a brief time working in a Philadelphia counting house, Hobart pursued Holy Orders, finding he deeply desired the ecclesiastical calling instead of a business career.[3] Hobart around this time started his collegiate education, initially attending the University of Pennsylvania before finishing his studies at Princeton. While studying theology for ordination purposes in New Jersey, he also served as a tutor—a mark of scholarly accomplishment.[4] Hobart expressed some concern about accepting the role of tutor, since it "then might be expected that I should join the Presbyterian communion."[5] He had no intention of so doing. However, he comported himself with distinction in this role and left this work still a committed Episcopalian.

In 1798, Hobart was ordained at Christ Church in Philadelphia to the office of deacon. The next several years involved short stays in

[1] John N. Norton, *The Life of Right Reverend John Henry Hobart, 2nd Edition* (New York: General Protestant Episcopal S. School Union, and Church Book Society, 1859), 1: 11.
[2] *Ibid.*, 12.
[3] See, for example, William Berrian, *Posthumous Works of the Late Rt. Rev. John Henry Hobart with a Memoir of the Life of the Right Reverend John Henry Hobart* (New York: Swords, Standford, and CO., 1833), 32-35.
[4] Norton, 19.
[5] John Henry Hobart, *Posthumous Works*, 1: 39.

16

various callings. Hobart served a year preaching and otherwise ministering at two small parishes near Philadelphia.[6] He then spent another year as rector of Christ Church in New Brunswick, New Jersey. After that, he ministered for a short period to a parish on Long Island. Though seemingly successful in all of these positions, Hobart did not appear content with his situation in any of them. His objections largely pertained to the amount of effort demanded in them and his own desire for time for further theological training and study. In December of 1800, he accepted a call as an assistant minister at Trinity Church in New York City. That same year, Hobart married Mary Goodwin Chandler, the daughter of another presbyter, Thomas Bradbury Chandler.[7] As with many influential and prominent bishops of the time, Hobart was reportedly blessed in this match by a virtuous and talented helpmeet. Hobart then was ordained into the priesthood the following year on April 5, 1801.

Part of Hobart's success in ministry came from his abilities in the pulpit. He proved a dynamic preacher, especially in contrast to the less affected style then common among American Episcopal clergy.[8] Early on in his career, he memorized his sermons, doing so in part due to his own eyesight issues. However, that method of preparation also proved effective for his delivery. Even later, when he no longer memorized his text, Hobart retained a familiarity with it that maintained his ability to give moving sermons. Throughout, his delivery was marked by a warmth and theatricality that drew comparisons to Methodism, both positively and negatively. His effective preaching partook of a broader ability to pastor those around him, including both laity and fellow clergy. This skill garnered much love toward himself and success in his broader ministry, drawing parishioners to be ministered by him and other clergy to minister with and under him.

Another early avenue of success came in published writing, which Hobart saw the usefulness of for furthering his ministerial goals.

---

[6] John McVickar, *The Professional Years of John Henry Hobart* (New York: Protestant Episcopal Press, 1836), 1.
[7] Norton, 24.
[8] Berrian, 79.

In his biography of Hobart, Norton comments that during this early period, few in the Protestant Episcopal Church used publication to inform and persuade parishioners and fellow clergy.[9] But Hobart was an exception. In 1804, he published "A Companion for the Altar." The same year his "A Companion for the Festivals and Fasts of the Church" also went to the presses. Both were devotional works revised and expanded from previous compositions by Church of England clergymen. Both went through many editions well after his death, garnering a significant audience instructed from Hobart's writings in the particulars of Episcopal worship.[10]

In his writings, Hobart also contributed to theological debates both with other churches and within his own. He became the undisputed leader of the "High Church" party within the Protestant Episcopal Church. Along both lines, among the most consequential works published in his lifetime was *An Apology for Apostolical Order and its Advocates* (1807).[11] In this volume, Hobart took on attacks against the episcopacy leveled by John M. Mason, then a prominent American Presbyterian and fierce defender of *de jure divino* Presbyterian government. Hobart countered that it was the Episcopal system which was of "divine authority," not the Presbyterian system. Thus, he went so far as to say that "a ministry not Episcopally ordained cannot be a valid ministry"[12] and to "commune with those who are not lawful ministers" was to be guilty of "the sin of schism."[13] Moreover, the lack of valid ministers also affected the ability of those in non-episcopal churches to be in "*visible* communion with Christ" through church ordinances.[14] At the same time, Hobart vigorously denied the accusation that he thought these "ministers" or the congregants of non-episcopal churches were not Christians. God would bless the efforts and accept the faith of those

---

[9] Norton, 29.
[10] See Gunn, 295.
[11] John Henry Hobart, *An Apology for Apostolic Order and Its Advocates* (New York: T.&J. Swords, 1807).
[12] *Ibid.*, 40.
[13] *Ibid.*, 42.
[14] *Ibid.*, 64.

who sincerely sought him, even if wrongly either through what Hobart termed "*unavoidable error*" or "*involuntary error*."[15] Though far from perfect, such persons still could have "*spiritual* communion with Christ" through a genuine faith.[16] These claims would put him in tension with some more ecumenical, Evangelical forces within his own church.

Here, Hobart also emphasized the continuity not just in theology but in physical descent from the Apostles to the present bishops of the Protestant Episcopal Church.[17] He then defended this episcopal government against Mason through "the only proper test," by which he meant the grounds of "scripture and antiquity."[18] These sources, he argued, more than adequately vindicated the necessity of episcopal government. He also spent considerable space pushing against the rhetorical approaches of his opponents, whom he accused of appealing to the "feelings" and thereby the "prejudice and passion" of readers. Instead, he wished to persuade them according to the cool dictates of reason.[19] This perspective on affections also would place him at odds with the increasing revivalism of American Christianity and its supporters within the Protestant Episcopal Church. His arguments here, written as a series of letters, proved a rallying cry for the episcopacy, one heralded and appealed to for decades to come in the Protestant Episcopal Church.

Moreover, Hobart showed a skill for organization. In 1809, he helped to found the "New York Bible and Common Prayer-Book Society." To these in New York he later would add "The Episcopal Tract Society," the "Young Men's Auxiliary Bible and Prayer-Book Society," the "New York Sunday School Society," the "Missionary" and "Education"

---

[15] *Ibid.*, 53-60. Unavoidable error he considered as applying to those who never even heard an argument for episcopacy. Involuntary he categorized as those who, though hearing it, remained genuinely unconvinced while still sincerely seeking God's will.

[16] *Ibid.*, 64.

[17] Kyle T. Bulthius, "Preacher Politics and People Power: Congregational Conflicts in New York City, 1810-1830" Church History 78(2)(June 2009): 265. See also Robert Bruce Mullin, Episcopal Vision/American Reality: High Church Theology and Social Thought in Evangelical America (New Haven: Yale University Press, 1986).

[18] Hobart, *An Apology*, 5.

[19] *Ibid.*, 6-8.

societies, and the Protestant Episcopal Press.[20] As with his other efforts, these endeavors bore fruit. From 1815 to 1817 alone, the number of Common Prayer books issued rose more than 400%.[21] These organizations helped in the development of parishes and the education of the laity as well. Hobart remained involved in these efforts throughout his bishopric, seeking to build structures that God could use to grow the Protestant Episcopal Church in holiness, knowledge, and numbers. Given the young and struggling state of the Episcopal Church when Hobart began his ministry, these efforts at institutional construction and development were crucial to its subsequent success in the United States.

In 1811, Hobart was selected as an assistant bishop in the diocese of New York. Benjamin Moore, who had shepherded the diocese for ten years as its second bishop, had been "struck by a partial paralysis" and said he could not fully fulfill the duties of his office without aid.[22] In addition to Bishop White, Bishops Provoost of New York and Jarvis of Connecticut participated in his consecration. He remained in service to a local parish as well, ministering at Trinity Church in New York City. There was some controversy, though, regarding his consecration. A local priest leveled accusations against his character. Though painful, these charges upon examination were not found credible. In fact, they ended up leading to the accusing priest's dismissal from Holy Orders. Furthermore, Bishop Provoost, the first bishop of New York, had been relieved of his jurisdiction over the state's parishes in 1801, replaced by Moore, due to health concerns. At the time leading up to Hobart's consecration, he sought to return to his post, possibly out of concern about the ecclesiastical leanings of the potential new assisting bishop. However, this attempt was gently but firmly rejected by a diocesan convention, who put out a statement that, while Provoost's consecration to the office of bishop was "indelible," he could and did resign his "jurisdiction"

---

[20] Norton, 43.
[21] Wilberforce, 313.
[22] Norton, 32.

over the New York diocese. That having been done in 1801, he could not of his own unilateral will take back up said jurisdiction.[23]

This event marked an important moment in the Protestant Episcopal Church. In his history of this church, Samuel Wilberforce called the consecration of Hobart nothing less than "a turning point in the history of the Western church."[24] Though hyperbolic, Wilberforce's statement did point toward the great influence the new bishop would wield. However, Hobart did not start off his momentous bishopric on easy grounds. As did other accomplished bishops at the time, Hobart found his diocese in sad shape. Much of the Protestant Episcopal Church in the early 19th century suffered from small numbers of parishioners, few clergy, and an ambivalent to antagonistic surrounding society.[25] New York was no different. To add to the monumental task, Bishop Moore quickly faded from active service, leaving the overwhelming share of diocesan care to Hobart.

Despite these challenges, Hobart succeeded greatly in growing the Diocese of New York. When he began, only 23 clergy served the entire Diocese. By the time of his death nineteen years later, that number had grown to 111.[26] Understanding the need for lasting foundations, Hobart succeeded here by committing his diocese and the broader Protestant Episcopal Church to training ministers. He desired not just more in ministry but a "learned as well as a pious ministry."[27] An important means for expansion came from the chartering of the General Seminary in 1817 in New York City. Clement C. Moore, son of the former New York Bishop and known to history for his poem, "A Visit from St. Nicholas," donated in trust a large portion of his estate for the erection

---

[23] William Stevens Perry, *History of the American Episcopal Church, 1587-1883* (Boston: James R. Osgood, 1883), 2: 159-161.
[24] Samuel Wilberforce, *A History of the Protestant Episcopal Church in America* (London: Levey, Robson, and Franklyn, 1844), 295.
[25] *Ibid.*, 303-304. See also Julien Gunn, "Bishop Hobart's Emphasis on Confirmation" *Historical Magazine of the Protestant Episcopal Church* 24(3)(September 1955): 294.
[26] Norton, 35.
[27] Quoted in E. Brooks Holyfield, *Theology in America* (New Haven: Yale University Press, 2003), 234.

PART I: VISIONARIES

of a place to train future clergy. This seminary was established to serve not just the Diocese of New York but, as its name would relay, the entire Protestant Episcopal Church. As a trustee of Colombia College, Hobart also wrested control of the institution's direction from a Presbyterian on the board and directed it toward more committed support for the Episcopal tradition.[28] Both the new and old educational institutions continued to display Hobart's impressive ability to build institutions to serve the Church.

Hobart also sought to expand the Protestant Episcopal Church in his diocese through missionary efforts. These endeavors included outreach to the Oneidas, a Native American tribe in Western New York. Hobart supported not only sending missionaries but also the translation of the Prayer Book into their language. This work proved successful and Bishop Hobart paid his first visit to them in 1818, confirming 89 at that time.[29] Hobart observed in relation to the visit, "We ought never to forget that the salvation of the Gospel is designed for all the human race, and that the same mercy which applies comfort to our wounded consciences—the same grace which purifies and soothes our corrupt and troubled hearts— and the same hope of immortality which fills us with peace and joy, can exert their benign and celestial influence on the humble Indian."[30] These Native Americans eventually would be removed to the area of Green Bay, Wisconsin, taking with them the faith God wrought through the efforts of Hobart and the Protestant Episcopal Church in New York.[31]

These accomplishments within the diocese of New York were impressive. But they hardly encapsulate Bishop Hobart's contribution.

---

[28] Wilberforce, *A History*, 305-306.
[29] Norton, 49-53.
[30] "Journal of the Proceedings of the Annual Convention of the Protestant Episcopal Church for the Diocese of New York for 1818," (New York: T. & J. Swords, 1818), 18-20.
[31] See Laurence M. Hauptman, L. Gordon McLester III and Judy Hawk, "Another Leatherstocking Tale: Susan Fenimore Cooper, The Episcopal Church, and the Oneida Indians" *New York History* 94(1-2)(Winter/Spring 2013): 9-39.

As leader of the High Church party,[32] Hobart sought to direct the American Episcopal Church toward his own camp. His work on the founding of the General Seminary was his most important effort on this front. Hobart molded and maintained the Seminary according to High Church principles. He also vigorously opposed the formation of other institutions for ministerial education by Evangelical or Low-Churchmen. While successful at building his own seminary, Hobart failed to stop institutions such as Kenyon in Ohio and Virginia Theological Seminary from also forming, comprising distinct and in certain ways competing centers of theological education within the Episcopal church.

Among his differences with Evangelical Low Churchmen, Hobart objected to how some discussed the *"invisible* Church" as a source of unity as undermining the need for visible unity. This visible unity he said accorded with the urgings found in St. Paul's epistles and the text of the ancient creeds.[33] The bishop also distinguished his views on baptism from those of the Evangelicals. Baptism involved "regeneration," whereby the baptized are "placed in a state of salvation in the Christian Church," through which they obtain "title to all the blessings and privileges of the Gospel covenant; and, as members of Christ's mystical body, the influences of the Holy Spirit, which animates that body, are pledged to us to enable us to fulfil our baptismal engagements." But Hobart distinguished this change of state from "renovation," which involved, "*change of heart and life* in the exercise of holy affections and in the practice of good works, through the influences of the Divine Spirit."[34] Regeneration could come without subsequent renovation. He thus denied the Roman view that the sacraments worked on the receiver merely by application (*opere operato*). However, he believed Low Church Evangelicals as well as other Protestants erred, too, in downplaying the efficacy of the objective action of receiving baptism.

[32] Holyfield, 236.
[33] John Henry Hobart, *The Corruptions of the Church of Rome Contrasted with Certain Protestant Errors* (New York: T&J Swords, 1818), 24-27.
[34] John Henry Hobart, *The Church Catechism* (New York: T&J Swords, 1819), 16.

PART I: VISIONARIES

Hobart also opposed most ecumenical efforts within and without his diocese. These efforts mostly came from Evangelicals seeking to join hands with members of other church denominations in parachurch and other structures. He objected, for instance, to any Episcopal Church participation in the American Bible Society, which formed in 1816. Many in his diocese wished to work with the organization, including Peter Jay, brother to the famous Founder John Jay, a firmly Evangelical Episcopal family. Hobart wrote a publicized letter against such efforts. He also engaged in his own expansive work to form societies similar to the ecumenical ones. Here his organizing skill, noted above, showed itself to great effect. He in part intended his various "societies" to serve as alternative routes to pursuing similar goals as the Evangelical party but without the interdenominational element.[35]

This position linked to another High Church priority. Hobart accused Evangelicals of insufficient fidelity to the Prayer Book with their divergences further encouraged by their ecumenical pursuits. Against claims that High Churchmen were guilty of *"formalism,"* Hobart responded by affirming "the ardor, zeal, and vigilance with which the High Churchman guards the prescribed worship of the Church."[36]

In defending these positions, Hobart was ready and even eager to point out the distinctives of the Protestant Episcopal Church in critiques of other Protestant denominations.[37] Frustrated, for example, by the revivalism taking hold in so much American Protestantism and even in elements of the Protestant Episcopal Church, Hobart emphasized the importance of the rite of confirmation, seeing it as an antidote to the Evangelical focus on personal conversion.[38] In line with his earlier work on the episcopacy, Hobart also decried the emotional elements of other

---

[35] Ibid., 267-269.
[36] John Henry Hobart, *A Word for the Church* (Boston: Stimpson and Clapp, 1832), 35.
[37] Frank E. Sugeno, "The Establishmentarian Ideal and the Mission of the Episcopal Church" Historical Magazine of the Protestant Episcopal Church 53(4)(December 1984): 287.
[38] See Gunn, 293-310.

manifestations of American religion, contrasting them with the sturdy groundings of the High Church particulars.

Bishop Hobart also pushed for the High Church position to be one that opposed engagement with the social and political sphere. He believed the Church should disengage from such debates, focusing more on the ministry of Word and Sacrament. In conformity with this commitment, Hobart also counseled against a growing Temperance Movement in the states. As alcoholic consumption rose in the first third of the 19th century, increasing calls came among Protestants for abstinence and even legal limitations, forerunners of the Prohibition movement that would pass the 18th Amendment in the early Twentieth Century. This debate did not occur in an ecclesiastical vacuum. It partook of broader issues within the Protestant Episcopal Church, which often split in its response to the Temperance Movement along Low/High Church lines. Evangelical or Low-Churchmen were more open to participating in the movement due to their greater engagement in social reform, their willingness to work in ecumenical organizations, and their openness to some elements of revivalism. Hobart, though cautioning for moderation in drinking, pushed against the Temperance Movement in part due to these other associations that went against his High Church principles.[39]

Though distinct from and in contention with the Low Church element of his day, Hobart's High Churchmanship should not be confused or conflated with the Anglo-Catholicizing brought on by the Oxford Movement. The New York diocese he did so much to form would prove among the more amenable to the influence of Newman, Pusey, and Keble. Yet that movement did not arise in any force in the United States till after Hobart's death. Moreover, he held views distinct from it, especially the form it took among those, like Newman, who eventually left the Church of England altogether. Surely with some of these debates then swirling in mind, Samuel Wilberforce declared of Hobart,

---

[39] See David M. Goldberg, "Drink Ye All of the This" Anglican and Episcopal History 89(1)(March 2020): 1-26.

"[h]e had no shrinking from the title Protestant, and was wholly free from the temper which confounds the maintenance of Church principles with a secret inclination towards the Romish communion."[40] He published extensive critiques of Roman Catholic beliefs and practices, declaring his church a Protestant one, even if one with distinctions from other denominations.[41] With the Church of England, the Protestant Episcopal Church held "her Articles of Faith, and her inestimable Liturgy."[42] After his death, the Hobart-wing of the Protestant Episcopal Church engaged in plenty of polemics against Rome, especially in the 1830s as an influx of Catholic immigrants came to the United States.[43] Thus, an accurate view of the High Church movement must recognize it as decidedly Protestant, a party that saw the Church of England and daughter churches as a distinct, and actually the best, manifestation of the Reformation.[44] This point matters in assessing Hobart, as later developments among some High Churchmen toward Oxford, including in the New York diocese, were not necessarily consistent with that bishop's own views.

Around 1822, Hobart suffered "a most violent attack of bilious fever,"[45] an ailment involving a fever brought on by too much bile or bilirubin in the blood. It often presented as jaundice. Though Hobart recovered this time, it foreshadowed not just later episodes but also his eventual demise. Shortly thereafter, Hobart went on a tour of foreign countries in pursuit of restoring his health. He traveled to Quebec where he suffered another violent episode. Still seeking some reprieve, he then left in the Fall of 1823 to visit England and Scotland. Hobart felt an especial kinship when visiting the latter land, in part due to the

[40] Wilberforce, 314.
[41] See Hobart, *The Corruptions of the Church of Rome*. See also Hobart, *A Word for the Church*.
[42] *Ibid.*, 13.
[43] Thomas Williams, "Early Hobartian Reaction to the Oxford Movement: Assessments of the 'Tracts for the Times' In 'The Churchman,' 1835-1841": 393-394.
[44] See George B. DeMille, The Catholic Movement in the American Episcopal Church (Philadelphia: The Church Historical Society, 1950), 9-14.
[45] Norton, 67.

Scottish church consecrating Bishop Seabury shortly after the American Revolution. Hobart also wrote back home extensively about the physical beauty of both England and Scotland, especially its rural landscapes. Hobart finally added Italy to his European travels before returning to New York in early October of 1825.[46]

By all accounts, Hobart seemed renewed from these travels and threw himself back into service to the diocese. He continued to consecrate churches and to ordain clergy. He confirmed many, including new additions to the church from the remaining Native American tribes. The Diocese of New York stood in a strong position internally and held a prominent place in the broader Protestant Episcopal Church.

During this time, Bishop Hobart partook of efforts in liturgical reform as well. In 1826, the Bishop led an effort to revise the Prayer Book on several fronts. First, he sought to shorten the Scripture readings for Morning and Evening Prayer. Among his reasons, Hobart intended these reforms in response to those who thought the services too long and to those ministers who already took measures to shorten the services but without any ecclesiastical approval.[47] He also sought to make clear that the different elements of the Ante-Communion service must be read, contrary to a (what he called "erroneous") reading of one of the rubrics in the service for Holy Communion. These efforts, then, were also about shoring up authority within the church by clarifying demands that clergy follow the rubrics of the Prayer Book entirely, even if doing so required some modification in the rubrics and rites themselves.

But Hobart's health continued to limit his capacities and, eventually, to shorten his days on earth. Another, this time fatal, fever attacked in the latter half of 1830. On September 2nd of that year, he preached his last sermon in Auburn, New York. The text was Job 28:28, "The fear of the Lord, that is wisdom." This passage also had been the text of his first sermon some thirty years prior.[48] He complained of chills

[46] Perry, 165-166; Norton, 75-77.
[47] Perry, 162-163.
[48] Norton, 89.

later that day and the fever took hold one last time, not to be sated but by its victim's death.

Hobart held on for another ten days, though in serious pain and decreasing strength. He was attended during this time by the Reverend Francis H. Cuming, then rector of St. Mark's in Grand Rapids, Michigan. Cuming had been visiting New York and sought out Hobart apart from knowing of his illness. Cuming records that, during his physical trial, Hobart expressed being overwhelmed by a sense of his own sinful unworthiness. Counseled by Cuming that "St. John saith, 'the blood of Jesus Christ cleanseth from all sin,'" Bishop Hobart replied, "O, yes, so he does, so he does. God be praised for that. God be praised for all his mercies."[49] He died on a Sunday, September 12th, at the age of 55.

Bishop Hobart was buried beneath the chancel of Trinity Church in New York City, the parish he had served so long during his broader shepherding of the diocese. His death was much lamented. A year after he passed, an entire book was published filled with sermons eulogizing the deceased bishop.[50] George Washington Doane, future bishop of New Jersey, preached one of them at Trinity Church in Boston. Doane had been ordained to the priesthood by Hobart and served for several years under him at Trinity in New York. Doane declared of Hobart, "His noble, elevated spirit, did not acknowledge, in its zealous efforts in the cause of truth and virtue, the limits of a single diocese, nor the claims of any one community: it soared the higher in its glorious flight, that it might thus dispense the wider good."[51] Published elsewhere, Benjamin Onderdonk, who would replace Hobart as Bishop of New York, lamented that, "[t]he cause of pure religion has been deprived of one of its most able and enlightened advocates and supporters."[52]

Hobart truly was an ecclesiastical giant of this period and remains a figure of great importance for understanding the history of

[49] Ibid., 94.
[50] *A Collection of Sermons on the Death of the Right Reverend John Henry Hobart* (New York: J.&T. Swords, 1831).
[51] Ibid., 179.
[52] Benjamin T. Onderdonk, *A Sermon Preached at the Funeral of the Right Reverend John Henry Hobart* (New York: Protestant Episcopal Press, 1830), 24.

the Protestant Episcopal Church. He led one of its most powerful parties, the shining star of American High Churchmanship. Beyond his own faction, he also did much to revive the Episcopal Church's fading prospects at one of its lowest points. His efforts included various fields– educating clergy, building supporting institutions, publishing devotional and polemical works, and missionary outreach to the lost. We owe the structural, intellectual, and moral vibrancy of the church in the 19th century in significant part to his efforts.

George Washington Doane
1799-1859

An ailing George Washington Doane mounted the prepared pulpit in the city hall of Burlington, New Jersey. Nearing sixty years old, Doane moved slowly, a testament not so much to any identifiable illness but to exhaustion and a general indisposition to care for himself physically. That particular February day in 1859, however, no matter how poorly he felt, Doane was determined to speak in person to a gathering of respectable women at city hall. The celebration was for the birthday of George Washington. Doane—Episcopal bishop of New Jersey—revered his namesake. He had been born just a few months before the great man died in Adventide of 1799, and Doane remained in awe of Washington throughout his life. The first president of the United States, Doane told his listeners, proved to be one of history's truly great men. Plutarch, Doane declared, "could write his lives in parallels; an illustrious Greek, by the side of an illustrious Roman: Theseus, with Romulus; Pericles, with Fabius Maximus; Aristides, with Cato Major; Alexander, with Julius Cæsar." Where, Doane asked, "shall the future Plutarch find his parallel, whose birthday twins, with that of the Republic?" Americans could find their republican hero in their own annals. "Next to the Fourth day of July, scarcely below it, in the calendar of patriotism, stands the twenty-second day of February." July fourth and February twenty-second were the two "great Festivals of thirty millions of free men." That day in February would be "through all the ages, next to the sacred anniversaries, the holy days of human nature. Who shall deny the legend, which our Eagle bears, to-day: 'ONE WORLD; ONE WASHINGTON!'" George Washington Doane, Episcopal Bishop, died two months later, his last major address having been an almost religious celebration of the United States' founding civil father.[1]

Doane ended his life celebrating the so-called Father of his country, an act appropriate for a bishop who made his mark welding the United States and the Episcopal Church into an ever-tightening embrace. Doane, more than any other Episcopal prelate in the first half of the Nineteenth Century, helped create the American civil religion that pervaded Episcopal Churches in the United States in the Nineteenth and Twentieth Centuries. Nations, he believed, were "Trustees, for the names of their great men. It is a sacred, it is a solemn, trust." A vociferous High Churchman, Doane believed that religious leaders as well as civil leaders had a duty to steward the reputations of a nation's great men. Doane spent his career working to create Christian patriots. A driven, ambitious man, Doane pushed his agenda in a manner that was always forceful and that sometimes was perceived as reckless. Money troubles at Burlington College, a denominational institution he founded ostensibly to educate Christian and more specifically Episcopal patriots, led to accusations of financial mismanagement. The house of bishops dismissed the charges, but the accusations soured Doane's relationship with Evangelicals who often found him imperious. Doane's desire to build defined his episcopacy. His patronage of architect Richard Upjohn helped instigate the Gothic revival that characterized Episcopal churches built after the middle of the Nineteenth Century. Doane's influence is hard to deny; Early Republic Episcopal Churches were more likely to be Low Church and made of wood. By 1900 they were more likely to be High Church and stone, largely because of Doane's activism and energy.[2]

---

[1] George Washington Doane, *One World, One Washington: The Oration, in the City Hall, Burlington, on Washington's Birth-day, 1859* (Burlington, NJ: Ladies' Mount Vernon Association, 1859), 5.
[2] Ibid.

The Doane family came from stolid English stock and settled in New Jersey. They were respectable, if not prominent. The future bishop's father, Jonathan, was a master builder and contractor who worked in the hinterland of New Jersey's capital city. Jonathan Doane died the year of his son's birth. Bereft of a father, Doane turned to his mother for nearly all of his emotional and spiritual needs. George W. Doane's son, William Croswell Doane, said that his father's "strongest points of character" came "through his Mother." Maternal guidance gave Doane his lifelong religiosity and his devotion to the Protestant Episcopal church as the truest expression of Christianity. Doane's mother was in her grandson's estimation "a noble woman, heroic, and self-denying; full of the wise instincts and great impulses of her nature; earnestly religious; and most careful and affectionate in the training of her children." Bishop Doane's Christian training received from his mother was not merely Christian, but deeply Anglican. "In days when the Church in America was weak and small, she had a brave woman's loyalty to its distinctive features." The distinctive features of Anglican churchmanship "molded, in no small degree, from early boyhood, the earnest promptness, and the bold uncompromising energy of character, that made him a 'defensor fidei' in life and death." Doane from childhood saw himself as a defender of a distinctively Anglican faith.[3]

Successive moves brought the Doane family to New York City and then to Geneva, New York on Lake Seneca. Doane's boyhood tutor was a Presbyterian clergyman, and even as a nine-year-old, Doane chafed at being forced to recite the Westminster Catechism. Doane defied the teacher and refused week after week to participate in the recitation. The chronology of Doane's willful anti-Westminster stand indicates that he saw his teacher as imposing Presbyterianism by a sort of educational fiat. His mother's staunch beliefs about episcopal churchmanship and the perceived (and very real) persecution that Episcopalians suffered in the aftermath of the American Revolution

---

[3] William Croswell Doane, *The Life and Writings of George Washington Doane* Volume 1 (New York: D. Appleton and Co., 1860), 11.

had been recited regularly to young George Doane, and he was not about to fail to defend the true faith in his schoolhouse. Westminster might be a catechism, but it was a catechism in error and he refused to recite it. Herein lay the roots of not only Doane's but other High Churchmen's intense dislike of Presbyterianism, which they regularly referred to as "Calvinism." William Croswell Doane related that "on the first catechising day, after my father went there, in answer to the question, 'What is the chief end of man?' he disavowed any knowledge of such a catechism." The defiant future bishop "utterly declined learning any other than the one his Mother had taught him. His determination was disobedience, and he suffered for it; being whipped and disgraced. But the spirit was not quelled." This was not a rejection of Reformational soteriology; what they objected to was the imposition of Presbyterian ecclesiology. Doane apparently convinced the other Episcopal boys to join him in the protest, and enough stood with him to force the hand of the undoubtedly exasperated Presbyterian teacher. [4]

Singular dedication to prelatical order defined Doane's commitment to the church. He continued his education at Union College in Schenectady, New York. Union's founders chartered the college as the first truly non-sectarian Christian institution of higher education in the United States but the school's institutional life remained influenced by Congregationalists and Presbyterians who dominated intellectual life in New England and Upstate New York. Always interested in religion and the church, he never became a sophisticated or systematic theological thinker. The Episcopal Church was his tribe, and his tribe was the true tribe. He pursued some theological training before his ordination to the diaconate in 1821, but he never had the same sort of training that other prelates, particularly those trained at Princeton, had before their own ordinations. The Episcopal Church inaugurated General Theological Seminary in 1817 but the seminary's impact remained limited to Episcopalians in and around New York City. John Henry Hobart, the theologically eccentric bishop of New York, ordained Doane as a presbyter in

[4] Doane, *The Life and Writings of George Washington Doane* Volume 1, 15.

1823. The younger man, like Hobart, romanticized the history of Anglican churches and pined for a connection of a historic church freed from the changes of the Nineteenth Century. Doane's devotion to the church was substantive, but it relied heavily on aesthetics of churchmanship. He told his sons that in preparation for ordination he "turned the current of his life towards the priesthood" and attended General Seminary. Doane never embraced theology as a vocation; his textbooks from the seminary were, his son William said, "without note or comment." He emulated John Henry Hobart in every way he could, and it was under Hobart's tutelage that Doane became a reflexive and not always thoughtful High Churchman. While in New York City Doane served at Trinity Church. Doane was a churchman before he was a theologian. But a churchman he was, and it is a testament to his devotion to the Episcopal Church that in 1832 the Episcopalians in his home state of New Jersey elected him their bishop.[5]

Bishops in the 1830s confronted the rise of Tractarianism in various ways. Evangelicals rejected it outright, but High Churchmen saw in the Tractarians a worthy if imperfect attempt to locate the ancient roots of their church in something more amenable to Anglican ecclesiology than the often Whiggish and anti-prelatical histories of the Reformation then in currency in the United States. Open curiosity about John Henry Newman's project typified High Churchmen in the 1830s. The *Tracts For the Times* divided Anglican opinion in Great Britain and in North America. Evangelicals, to their credit, saw the more vehement devotees of Newman as openly questioning Reformational commitments to Protestant soteriology. Doane never seemed interested in controversies related to the mechanisms of salvation. His defense of Tractarianism rested in his belief that Anglican churches—defined as a church founded in England by the apostles, ruled by episcopal successors to the apostles, and reformed in the Sixteenth Century—were the true Church. Doane therefore relied more on the sympathies of the broad

---

[5] Powel Mills Dawley, *The Story of the General Theological Seminary: A Sesquicentennial History, 1817–1967* (Oxford: Oxford University Press, 1999), 73; Doane, *Life and Writings...* Vol 1, 27.

Tractarian project and less on Newman's specific personal battle with a Protestant reading of history. Doane nonetheless cast his lot openly with the Tractarians even as he tried to rescue them from their excesses. He edited, for example, an early American edition of John Keble's *The Christian Year*. His defense of Tractarians extended to sympathizers who remained in Anglican churches, and it was Doane's unconditional commitment to episcopal ecclesiology and apostolic succession that convinced him to fight Evangelical enemies of the Tractarian movement. [6]

In 1834 prominent Protestant intellectuals in the United States accused Tractarians of trying to roll back the gains of the Reformation, and of closeted Roman Catholicism. Princeton-trained minister and seminary professor Henry A. Boardman openly accused Episcopal and Church of England rectors and theologians of returning to the worst excesses of what Boardman called Popery. Boardman termed "the present religious state of Great Britain" "ominous" and warned that unless the Evangelicals regained leadership of the Church of England, "The Oxford Tract movement" would lead the Church of England towards "Romanism." Boardman did not see much hope for the English Church though because "a large and learned body of the clergy, (embracing the leading ecclesiastical teachers at the ancient University of Oxford) have returned to some of the worst errors of Popery." Tractarianism, Boardman warned, employed "both the pulpit and the press with prodigious efficiency, to give them currency among the people." Boardman, along with prominent Low Churchmen like assistant bishop William Meade of Virginia, Charles Pettit McIlvaine of Ohio, and Evangelical-minded broad churchmen like Bishop Alexander Viets Griswold of Massachusetts warned that any controversy beginning in Anglican Great Britain would inevitably make its way to the United States and would, feared Boardman, "operate powerfully upon this country." What Boardman and Evangelical Episcopalians believed was a potential increase of "Romanism" in the United Kingdom "can hardly fail of giving a fresh

---

[6] Lawrence N. Crumb, "American Reflections on the Oxford Movement: Two Unpublished Letters." *Anglican and Episcopal History* 59, no. 1 (1990): 99–107.

impulse to it here." Boardman worried that the "Oxford Tract leaven is already beginning to work in our cities; and Roman Priests are publicly felicitating their people on the progress their doctrines are making in the bosom of a Protestant church."[7]

Doane represented the majority of High Churchmen in the United States who sympathized with the Tractarians when he argued against Boardman's characterization of the so-called Oxford Movement as closeted Catholicism. He told Boardman that the Episcopal Church was a "sister church" to Presbyterians and resented the suggestion that Tractarians had ceased to be Protestant. Doane believed that the Tractarians, far from being a vehicle for converts to make their way to Roman Catholicism, were an important bulwark against potential conversions. Doane told Boardman and other detractors that he did not "identify myself with any school or set of men, on either side of the Atlantic." He defended the men who Boardman "charged as striving to pervert their age to Popery." The supposed closet Romanists, Doane said, professed "to stand upon the ground which Cranmer held at his life's cost, the ground of primitive antiquity." The Tractarians were men whose "talents, learning, piety, integrity, holiness, heavenly-mindedness and charity… would adorn the purest age the Church has ever known." More importantly, Doane said that Roman Catholics understood what Boardmen could not: that the Tractarians were "the boldest and the ablest living champions of the truth, against the force and fraud of fallen, frenzied Rome." [8]

Theological controversy never formed the core of Doane's ministry. From the time he became bishop in 1832 he worked tirelessly to weld Episcopal churchmen into committed American patriots. As late as the War of 1812 some Episcopal rectors and even several bishops held

[7] George Washington Doane, *A Brief Examination of the Proofs by which the Rev. Mr. Boardman Attempts to sustain His charge that "A Large and Learned Body of the Clergy of the Church" (of England) "Have Returned to Some of the Worst Errors of Popery;" With a Word or Two As to His Attempt, Without Proof to Cast the Suspicion of Popery on the Protestant Episcopal Church in the United States of America* (Burlington, NJ: J.L. Powell, 1841), 10.

[8] Doane, *A Brief Examination*, 5, 10.

the revolutionary legacy of the United States at arm's length. Doane felt no such ambiguity about the origins of the American republic and he celebrated it throughout his prelacy. Fundamentally, Doane not only wanted Episcopalians to celebrate the United States; he wanted them to lead it. He conceived of patriotic expression as a necessary Christian duty and took every opportunity to remind students at Burlington College that they had what he called "geographic" obligations. "It cannot be questioned, for a moment," he told Burlington College students in 1853, "that there are geographical responsibilities." Various "peculiarities of position, peculiarities of climate, peculiar political institutions, historical peculiarities create, continue, and enforce, local relations and national duties." He reiterated that patriotism was "in a word, GEOGRAPHICAL RESPONSIBILITIES" that every patriot owed their respective country. Doane recalled "the sentiment of that old Laconian adage… Sparta is your birthplace: make it your pride to honor it." Patriotism "kindled in St. Paul's great heart, when, to the chief captain at Jerusalem, who gloried in the Roman citizenship, which he had obtained, for 'a great sum,' he answered, with sublime sententiousness, 'But I was born free!'" Doane struck a particularly Anglican note when he reminded his listeners how patriotism "blazed, in those few burning words, which old Hugh Latimer spoke, to his brother Bishop, at the stake, 'Be of good cheer, Master Ridley, and play the man; we shall this day light such a candle, by God's grace, in England, as shall never be put out.'" Patriotism was the "very spirit of what David sang to his angelic harp, in that proudest pæan, which patriotism ever prompted: 'Jerusalem is built as a city, that is at unity in itself.'" Doane did not posit a sort of racial or even national patriotism, but one predicated on divinely ordered human flourishing. The biblical injunction to "pray for the peace of Jerusalem" was patriotic. So too was the hope that one's own city or country would prosper. Love, not power, compelled Christians to hope that peace would reign "within thy walls, and plenteousness within thy palaces." It was for the sake of others—"For my brethren and companions' sakes"—that Americans wished prosperity upon their own land and their fellow people. "The sentiment, of which I speak," declared Doane, "with its resulting duties and responsibilities, is as true of America, as it ever was of Sparta, Rome or England."⁹

Concern for patriotic Christianity was not in Doane's imagination a secular or worldly pursuit. Like most Episcopal churchmen of the Nineteenth Century, he did not affirm the division of temporal and religious society into two kingdoms in the way that early Twenty-first Century Americans Evangelicals do. This did not mean he was a proponent of theocracy. Doane, like all of the prelates of the Episcopal Church consecrated in the Nineteenth Century, remained a convinced disestablishmentarian. But disestablishment did not require religion and politics to be strictly separated, and Doane believed he had a duty to not only speak to the civil order, but to do so regularly. And he did. There was in the United States and in the Nineteenth Century, Doane lamented, "a growing tendency to separate between things sacred and things secular, in point of obligation." Americans in the Nineteenth Century, he warned, placed "on the field of human life, a line of higher, and a line of lower duties" that led to the adoption of "a sort of 'sliding scale' in morals." This faux division, remarked Doane, meant that that religion became "a thing of Sundays, and of sermons, and of sacraments, alone; and not of every day's concern, and of our universal life."¹⁰

Religion's influence in American society and in American civic life became a paramount concern for Doane. The creation of Burlington College and Doane's near-constant public speaking on religious and patriotic subjects showed his commitment to making the United States a more Christian society. Doane's devotion was always passionate but not always careful, and the finances of Burlington College were controversial enough that some of his fellow bishops suspected him of

---

9　George Washington Doane, *The Young American, His Dangers, His Duties, & His Destinies: The Address at Burlington College, July 4, 1853...the Seventh Anniversary of the Founding of Burlington College* (Philadelphia: Inquirer Press, 1853), 7.
10　George Washington Doane, *Civil Government a Sacred Trust from God: The Anniversary Oration Before the New Jersey State Society of Cincinnati, At Trenton, July 4ᵗʰ, MDCCCXLV* (Burlington, NJ: Edmund Morris, 1845), 9-10.

ineptitude at best and malfeasance at worst. Doane's open dislike of Evangelicals, his partisan wrangling with bishops less sympathetic to Tractarians, and his flirtation with material opulence did not help his cause, and in 1852 three bishops filed a presentment against Doane. The three bishops—Charles Petit McIlvaine of Ohio, William Meade of Virginia, and George Burgess of Maine—filed their charges after laymen in the diocese of New Jersey complained to them about how Doane stewarded church finances. The ostensible reason was Doane's handling of Burlington College's finances but the insinuation was that Doane generally acted like an authoritarian in his diocese. The accusing bishops implied that Doane racked up large debts—undoubtedly true—and that he did not carefully distinguish between diocesan finances and his personal money. An assembly of bishops cleared Doane of wrong-doing after a trial convened and then dismissed the charges in the fall of 1852. The presenting bishops did not pursue any other charges but it is likely that Doane was quickened enough by the experience to tread more carefully with diocesan monies and resources. His building program slowed down precipitously in the 1850s, but his influence on church architecture was unmistakable. Richard Upjohn was commissioned by other churchmen in the years that followed.[11]

Bishop Doane coupled intellectual construction of American patriots with the construction of actual buildings. His father had been a contractor and a builder and in many ways the fever for construction never left the son. Doane's fellow bishops from socially elite backgrounds and families like Virginia patrician William Meade, Anglo-Irish patrician John Henry Hopkins of Vermont, or Charles Pettit McIlvaine, carefully cultivated public images predicated on modest dress and middle-class

---

[11] Robert W. Prichard, *A History of the Episcopal Church* (New York: Morehouse Publishing, 2014), 187; An exhaustive account of the accusations against Doane can be found in *The Record of the Proceedings of the Court of Bishops: Assembled for the Trial of George Washington Doane D.D., LL. D., Bishop of New Jersey upon a Presentment made by The Rt Revd William Meade D.D. Bishop of Virginia, The Rt Revd Charles Petit McIlvaine D.D., Bishop of Ohio, and the Rt Rev George Burgess D.D., Bishop of Maine* (New York: Stanford and Sword, 1857).

social habits despite being the scion of a Virginia planter family, the landholding Protestant ascendancy in Ireland, and the son of a United States Senator, respectively. Doane, the son of a middling builder, saw no reason to restrain his penchant for magnificent construction projects. At times his affinity for the magnificent flirted with opulence. He commissioned Scottish-born Philadelphia architect John Nottman to design a large Italianate residence for his family. Nottman and Doane collaborated again when Doane wanted a home for girls built by the Episcopal diocese of New Jersey. Doane's most enduring, famous, and most important architectural collaboration joined his reputation with that of Richard Upjohn. English-born Upjohn made his name by designing and promoting neo-Gothic style in the American republic at a time when the increasingly prosperous Protestant churches in the United States wanted more substantive buildings than the quaint and beautiful but generally humble churches they worshiped in the Colonial and Early National eras. Upjohn's architectural preferences entranced Doane. The bishop of New Jersey's romantic vision of a sturdy church that had endured from the time of the apostles to the creation of the American Union needed buildings to awe communicants, and Upjohn was just the man to deliver. The architect built Doane's home parish, St. Mary's in Burlington, New Jersey. The Gothic style structure still stands 170 years later. Doane's wife, Eliza, hailed from a family of affluent Bostonians and she helped him raise money and finance his building projects. Their stately home on the banks of the Delaware became a sort of salon for High Churchmen. Doane's two sons drank deeply from the paternal well and both became convinced High Churchmen. William Croswell served as the first bishop of Albany from 1869 to 1913. His brother George Hobart Doane drank perhaps a bit too deeply the High Church well, and converted to Roman Catholicism in 1855.[12]

Controversy and devotion defined Doane as a man and as a bishop. Never one to shy away from a fight, he earned his share of friends

---

[12] Brian Regan, *Gothic Pride: The Story of Building a Great Cathedral in Newark* (Piscataway, NJ: Rutgers University Press, 2012), 73

and enemies in his nearly three decades as a bishop. His popularity with patriotic clerics of all denominations was undeniable, however, and the public addresses that occurred at his death in 1859 were given not only by Episcopalians but by Presbyterians as well. Doane called a Princeton Seminary professor "a distinguished laborer and faithful friend." When a mutual friend of Doane and Hodge died in 1845, Hodge sent word to the bishop through a friend: "I have been thinking of Bishop Doane, and should like to see him, and wish him to know it." Courtland Van Rensselaer, the minister of the Presbyterian church in Burlington, decided to preach a funeral sermon for Doane when he heard the news. Whatever disagreements Doane had with this particular Presbyterian, they did not keep Van Rensselaer from considering him a friend. Doane, the Presbyterian argued, was like every man imperfect, but that did not mean that Doane was guilty of the accusations and insinuations made by his own church and by others in the years since his 1852 trial. "In the first place, Bishop Doane's most intimate friends believed him innocent." Other people who knew him—"judges, lawyers, physicians, divines, intimate acquaintances, male and female, by scores and thousands—placed the most implicit confidence in his motives and integrity." The Episcopal Church, Van Rennselaer reminded his church, "in its Diocesan and General Convention, was never against him. Indeed the House of Bishops formally declared his innocence; and this is presumptive proof that his religious character could not be impugned in the Church to which he belonged." Van Rensselaer believed that God had given Doane a vote of confidence. It cannot be denied that God showed no little favor to the Bishop in life and in death. He enabled him to accomplish a large amount of good; protected him in Providence from a varied and powerful opposition; and permitted him, after a long life of labor and trial, to die in peace." Although these "three facts, just mentioned," did not amount to an absolute demonstration of Doane's innocence, they certainly, Van Rensselaer argued, could not be ignored. "To a person, like myself, outside of his Church, and an unexcited observer of passing events in the community, they afford evidence of no slight character." Doane's episcopacy does not present an overwhelmingly positive picture of pastoral care, but he undoubtedly left a mark on the Episcopal church through his championing of High Churchmen and his enthusiasm for neo-Gothic architecture. By 1900, Gothic Episcopal churches like Trinity Church Boston and the behemoth Cathedral of St. John the Divine in New York City increasingly typified sacred spaces commissioned by Episcopalians. High Churchmen also undoubtedly were in the ascendant particularly in New Jersey and in New York. Bishop Doane Doane was many things, but Van Rensselaer was undoubtedly correct when he defined his Episcopal friend as "no slight character." [13]

---

[13] William Croswell Doane, *The Life and Writings of George Washington Doane* Volume 4 (New York: D. Appleton and Co., 1861), 364; Courtland Van Rensselaer, *A Funeral sermon on the occasion of the death of Bishop Doane. Preached in the Presbyterian Church, Burlington, N.J., On May 1st 1859* (Philadelphia: J.M. Wilson 1859), 6.

Part II

Missionaries

Jackson Kemper
1789-1870

At the Episcopal Church's general convention in 1835, the bishops gathered to send one of their number as a missionary bishop to what was then called the Northwest. The hierarchs of the Episcopal Church had good reason, they believed, to dispatch a missionary bishop to the western states. The rapid rise of revivalist sects borne out of the Second Great Awakening and the surprising success of groups like Joseph Smith Jr's Church of Jesus Christ of Latter Day Saints convinced the Episcopal prelates that something had to be done. Methodists and Presbyterians had some presence in the western states and those groups retained some form of a true church but the Arminianism of the Methodists and the truncated ecclesiology of the Presbyterians could not represent the one true apostolic church against revivalist anarchy and Roman Catholic usurpation to Americans in the Western states. Many settlers in the Northwest had never been admitted to the Lord's Supper or even baptized. It was a moral and religious necessity to send a missionary bishop to the Northwest. The man the bishops chose, Jackson Kemper, subtly succeeded in his mission not only as a missionary churchman who hoped to save souls, but also as a religious leader bent on civilizing a portion of what became the modern Midwest through the creation of churches, schools, a seminary, and philanthropic organizations.

The United States Kemper entered at his birth found the republic still in its infancy. Upstate New York was less than a decade out of the

PART II: MISSIONARIES

Revolutionary War. President George Washington and congress governed the still new American republic from New York City. Cholera, diphtheria, malaria, typhoid, and dozens of other diseases ravaged the city. The municipality's residents regularly endured outbreaks of sickness that convinced sizable numbers of its 33,000 denizens to flee up the Hudson River Valley to healthier climes. It was during one of these semi-regular outbreaks that Daniel and Elizabeth Kemper left what is now lower Manhattan and made a temporary home in newly-formed Columbia County, across the Hudson River from the Catskill Mountains. The Kempers—Anglicans, despite Elizabeth's Dutch Reformed heritage—welcomed their son Jackson on Christmas Eve, 1789. [1]

Daniel Kemper—a devoted Episcopal churchman and Revolutionary War veteran who served as an officer and sutler in the Continental Army—sent his son to the Episcopal Academy at Cheshire, Connecticut at the age of twelve. Young Jackson, shy, somewhat withdrawn by nature, and prone to being bullied by a rowdy set of boys who dominated life at the academy, emotionally withered at Cheshire. Daniel Kemper withdrew his son and employed an Anglo-Irish tutor, a Church of Ireland priest named Edmund Barry, to finish Jackson's education. Jackson flourished and managed to gain admittance to Columbia College in New York City just after he turned sixteen years old. When he graduated—as valedictorian—he spent a year doing theological study, largely under the influence of John Henry Hobart. Kemper drank up Hobart's High Churchmanship and remained a committed High Churchman throughout his life. But Kemper also never had Hobart's hard-edged dislike of Evangelicals. This was undoubtedly because he began his studies under Hobart's broad-church predecessor, Benjamin Moore. Bishop Moore was described as "a true, consistent, and…an uncompromising Episcopalian," but was not "an aggressive or prescribing one." Moore remained more welcoming to non-Anglicans during his tenure as president of Columbia College, and sought irenic

---

[1] Hermon Griswold Batterson, *A Sketch-book of the American Episcopate* (Philadelphia: J.B. Lippincott & Co., 1878), 117.

relationships with Protestant intellectuals in New York City. Moore's influence over Kemper meant that Kemper managed to carry his High Churchmanship without the sectarian dogmatism of Hobart. Kemper completed his studies in 1811, and Bishop William White ordained him as a deacon that same year in Philadelphia's St.Peter's Church. Three years later, he became a presbyter.[2]

From the outset of his ministry, Kemper's interest in missionary work defined his conception of his vocation. During the War of 1812 he began working as an itinerant priest in the far western reaches of Pennsylvania and New York. Kemper served the bishops of New York throughout the 1820s. In 1831, he became the rector of St. Paul's Church in Norwalk, Connecticut. The convention of 1835 that elected him as a missionary bishop was a turning point in the history of the Episcopal Church for a variety of reasons, and the creation of a missionary bishopric in the Old Northwest remains one of its most enduring legacies. Because of Kemper, the liturgical and ecclesiastical culture of the Episcopal Church's domestic missionary enterprises became and remained distinctively High Church, even as the denomination's largest dioceses—Massachusetts, Ohio, South Carolina, and Virginia—took on the Evangelical character of their bishops. Kemper's jurisdiction took in every western state north and west of the Ohio River with the exception of the states of Ohio and Illinois, where Philander Chase served as bishop. Modern Iowa, Indiana, Michigan, Minnesota, Missouri, and Wisconsin all were under Kemper's charge; the sheer geographic size of Kemper's jurisdiction meant that he was well-positioned to affect the churchmanship of what became nearly half a dozen dioceses in the three decades that followed his prelacy. Although Kemper's charge gave him a massive territory and he understandably traveled regularly, he followed

---

[2] Howard Morris Stuckert, "Jackson Kemper, Presbyter." *Historical Magazine of the Protestant Episcopal Church* 4, no. 3 (1935): 130–51; John B. Pine, "Benjamin Moore, S.T.D." *Columbia University Quarterly* II (June 1900): 259–261; Greenough White, *An Apostle of the Western Church: Memoir of the Right Reverend Jackson Doctor of Divinity, First Missionary Bishop of the American Church with Notices of some of His Contemporaries* (New York: Thomas Whittaker, 1900), 2.

PART II: MISSIONARIES

the custom of holding the rectorship of a parish. Kemper resided in St. Louis throughout his prelacy, and served as the rector of Christ Church in that city.[3]

The establishment of an episcopate in the Northwest displayed something on The Episcopal Church's ambivalent relationship with the idea of the frontier in general. Certainly the dozen or so bishops who made up the Episcopal hierarchy had no interest in seeing their church beholden to revivalists sects who were hardly orthodox to begin with, nor did they want to cede the frontier Northwest to Baptists and Methodists with their uneducated preachers who prayed on the equally uneducated and non-catechized citizens of the Northwest. The Episcopal bishops also understood that they had a mission to a place that was not merely religious; it was patriotic as well. The late Walter Nugent, a well-regarded historian of the American West, empire, and frontier who taught at the University of Indiana and Notre Dame, noted in his *Habits of Empire* that Americans' relationship with the frontier was a patriotic wedding of republican values with a divine mission to fulfill "the plans of God and Nature for America." This has been rendered as Manifest Destiny. Historians have attached the origins of Manifest Destiny to New England Puritanism, and with good reason. The Puritan Calvinist typology concerning the relationship between God and His people meant that New Englanders easily put themselves in the place of the Ancient Israelites; North America was the Canaan to be conquered and ordered to the true worship of God. Timothy Dwight IV, president of Yale College between 1795 and 1817, famously wrote an epic poem, *The Conquest of Canaan*, that probed these themes for a new generation of American Protestants. There is no reason whatsoever to think that Episcopalians in the Early National United States did not share Puritan conceptions of the relationship to the church, the people of God, and the West. Walter Nugent notes that "diverse American voices—religious,

[3] Walter Herbert Stowe, "A Turning Point: The General Convention of 1835." *Historical Magazine of the Protestant Episcopal Church* 4, no. 3 (1935): 152–79; Frederick Cook Morehouse, *Some American Churchmen* (Milwaukee, WI: The Young Churchman Co., 1892), 110.

cultural, and economic—converged in the assumption that Transappalachia was and had to be American." Kemper's mission, therefore, was to try and ensure that at least some of the settlers living west of the Appalachian Mountains would be Protestant Episcopalians.[4]

The circumstances of Kemper's consecration confirmed the wedding of Episcosopal churchmanship with a healthy dose of civil religion. The preacher, New Jersey Bishop George Washington Doane, was foremost among his peer prelates in his unparalleled zeal in making Anglicanism the preferred religion of American republican high culture. Doane painted a picture of western states devoid of true religion and, by proxy, civilization if Kemper failed to convert settlers and plant true churches in the region. "Through the regions of our own unbounded West see how the stream of life sets onward. Behold, in arts, in wealth, in power, a progress such as earth has never seen, outrunning even fancy's wildest dreams." The settlement of the West, Doane warned, was proceeding without "provision that at all keeps pace with it, for the securing of man's nobler and immortal interests." The American West was populating, but Protestant churches were not keeping pace. He lamented the "keen and shrewd regard the Church of Rome has marked that region for her own, and with what steadiness of purpose she pursues her aim; and seeks to lay the deep foundations of a power which is to grow as it grows, and to strengthen as it gathers strength." Kemper and his fellow bishops believed that Anglicanism represented the best chance of making the American West civilized and Protestant. It also represented the best chance of fending off heterodox revivalism of Second Great Awakening-influenced Calvinist and Evangelical sects cropping up in nascent communities in western states "The Church of England," declared Doane, "long by God's protecting favour, the stay and hope of Christendom, now needs her utmost succours for her own defence against the

---

[4] Anders Stephenson, *Manifest Destiny: American Expansion and the Empire of Right* (New York: Hill and Wang, 1995), 6-8; Timothy Dwight IV, *Conquest of Canaan; A Poem in Eleven Books* (Hartford, CT: Elisha Babcock, 1785); Walter Nugent, *Habits of Empire: A History of American Expansion* (New York: Alfred A. Knopf, 2008), 22-23.

impious combination that attempts her overthrow." That impious combination was formed by revivalist and Roman Catholics. "The Christian brethren, not of our communion, who have seemed to grow and multiply about us with a vigour so prolific," had begun to feel and own, "the want of those inherent principles of union which alone can bind in one large masses of mankind." Revivalist sects were "destitute of ancient landmarks," which made them "stray insensibly from 'the old paths,' in which alone God's promise gives assurance of protection and of peace." Believers who passed through revivalist churches "turn instinctively to us. They recognize the doctrines which we hold, as the old faith which once was given to the Saints."[5]

Kemper, like Doane, devoted himself to more than one faith. The new missionary bishop for the Old Northwest was a convinced Episcopalian in religion, and a devoted Federalist in his politics. "Politically, he was bred in the Federal school, and was never known to express dislike of any one as emphatically as of Thomas Jefferson." Kemper's distaste for Jefferson was such that even friends who praised him for his general moderation noted that his criticism of Jefferson could border on being unrestrained. Kemper's Federalism was not that of New England's High Federalists, however. His primary biographer noted that "he inherited from his New York Dutch ancestry and connections their longstanding prejudice against New England." Kemper's mission conjoined the proclamation of the Gospel, the furtherance of the United States' republican society, and the Federalist and subsequently Whig visions of expansion of Christian civilization that wedded Christian social reform with societal progress. Doane told Kemper, "it is the pledge of God that he will hear, that he will bless, that he will save his Church, placed thus upon the vantage ground of Christendom, and made—I speak it without the fear of contradiction— the Missionary Church of the whole world." Now, intoned Doane, it was Kemper's duty

[5] George Washington Doane, *The Missionary Bishop: The Sermon at the Consecration of The Right Reverend Jackson Kemper, D.D., Missionary Bishop for Missouri and Indiana; in St. Peter's Church, Philadelphia, September 25, 1835* (Burlington, NJ: J. L. Powell, 1835), 11-13.

to "go on, as you have now begun, in the benign and blessed impulse of that Missionary spirit which God has poured upon his Church."⁶

The American West of the 1830s, particularly the Old Northwest, had little in the way of cultural or social foundations on which to base an Episcopal diocese. Episcopalians on the ground were non-existent, and even getting to the territory which he was to spiritually oversee forced Kemper to endure the most rudimentary forms of travel. In his first year he rode episcopal visitations in wagons, often sitting with livestock in hay as he made his way to far-flung homes of would-be communicants and parishioners. One occasion on a flatboat falling temperatures threatened to lock the small craft in ice in the bitter cold with no shelter nearby. The terrified passengers watched as the bishop joined the boat's crew in breaking up the ice floes surrounding the flatboat. Given the relative hardship of the assignment, and the fact that Kemper left few published works for a churchman of his stature, the reasons that attracted Kemper are left to the historian's conjecture. There is some reason to believe that Kemper's interest in Native Americans compelled him to assume a post that placed him in relatively close contact with indigenous peoples. Black Hawk's War, which pitted the U.S. Army against warriors of the Sac and Fox nation under the command of their eponymous chief, ended three years before Kemper made his way to Indiana. The publication of Indian memoirs like Black Hawk's influenced opinion in New England. Kemper, a resident of Connecticut at the time of his election, would have been familiar with Native Americans who converted to Christianity at institutions like Moore's Indian Charity School in Lebanon, Connecticut. Katherine Jeanne Gallagher, a professor of history at Goucher College during the first half of the Twentieth Century, speculated that the diocese of New York's longtime relationship with the resident New York Indians prompted Kemper's interest in ministry with Native Americans. ⁷

---

6   Stuckert, "Jackson Kemper, Presbyter," 130–51.; George Washington Doane, *The Missionary Bishop*, 27.
7   Katharine Jeanne Gallagher, "Bishop Jackson Kemper and the Northwest Mission" PhD diss. (University of Wisconsin-Madison, 1915), 45-46; J.B.

PART II: MISSIONARIES

A probable mix of interest in ministry to Indians, concerns over the rise of revivalism and Roman Catholicism, and a general disposition to heed a perceived call to ministry from God combined to compel Kemper towards the setting sun and become a missionary bishop. Kemper did not go west with passive or unformed expectations about what type of church needed to be set up in the western states of the American Union. Kemper, like most of Hobart's disciples, believed that true churches were those episcopal churches that affirmed the necessity of the rule of bishops, the principle of apostolic—although not Petrine—succession, and that affirmed baptismal regeneration. Kemper, put simply, was a convinced High Churchman. Kemper's sympathies led him to be an effective champion for Anglican distinctives on the frontier, but also to injudiciously support Benjamin T. Onderdonk when the latter's scandalous tenure as bishop of New York eventually led to a succession of church trials. Onderdonk clumsily implied Roman Catholic sympathies when he decided to defend Arthur Carey, a London-born twenty-one year old curate who pushed a brand of ritualism that proved to be too radical for most rectors in New York City. A series of women also accused Onderdonk of inappropriate advances towards them. Kemper most likely saw Onderdonk as a victim of Evangelical witch hunts. Like Onderdonk, Kemper learned his brand from the tutelage of Bishop Hobart, and Kemper understandably believed he was simply defending a fellow New Yorker and High Churchman. [8]

Bishop Kemper's own tenure as a prelate was nearly immaculate. He managed—despite significant financial, cultural, and social difficulties—to build a substantive ministry to Indians in the Old Northwest and to create educational institutions that stood the test of time.

Patterson ed., *Life of Black Hawk, Or Ma-ka-tai-me-she-kia-kiak* (London: Richard James Kennett, 1836); James Dow McCallum, ed., *The Letters of Eleazar Wheelock's Indians* (Hanover, N.H.: Dartmouth College Publications, 1932).

[8] E. Clowes Chorley, "Benjamin Tredwell Onderdonk, Fourth Bishop of New York." *Historical Magazine of the Protestant Episcopal Church* 9, no. 1 (1940): 1–51; Patricia Cline Cohen, "Ministerial Misdeeds: The Onderdonk Trial and Sexual Harassment in the 1840s." *Journal of Women's History* 7, no. 3 (1995): 34-57.

He also dealt with the sometimes-contentious episcopal politics of the day deftly, without personal pretense. Kemper knew himself to be "not a great man intellectually, not a thinker, scholar, writer or eloquent preacher. Such is the testimony of one who knew him best and loved him most, and none was better aware of these facts than he himself." The missionary bishop had "the most modest views of his powers and attainment." Kemper's modesty certainly gave him an advantage when dealing with his brother bishops in the region, particularly the authoritarian and often imperious bishop of Ohio, Philander Chase. When Chase publicly implied that Kemper had an abnormally large personal income from his salary and other church funds, Kemper responded moderately and took the time to explain in relative detail the sources of his personal finances. When Owen Lovejoy, brother of murdered abolitionist Elijah Lovejoy, attempted to gain the public support of the Episcopal Church for abolitionist politics and reforms, Kemper rejected the church's participation in any activity that might be conceived as potentially partisan. The subject of abolition, he argued, was "an exceedingly exciting one, and is necessarily connected with the politics of the country." In his capacity as bishop, however, Kemper refused to engage in the politics of abolition, which he sympathized with. "The kingdom of the Redeemer is not of this world," wrote the bishop, and as a ministering servant of Christ he had "enough to do to teach men the principles by which they should be regulated and the duties which result from their various and sacred relations in life." If the church went further and attempted "to influence or control the operations of Government we shall do that for which we can plead the sanction neither of our Lord nor of his apostles."[9]

While Kemper disliked the idea of the church doing partisan politics, he was not indifferent to the need for the church to act politically in substantive ways. The American Great West was a civilizational tabula rasa, with little cultural or social history to build a successful Episcopal church on. Yet it was the very emptiness of the Old Northwest

---

[9] Greenough White, *An Apostle of the Western Church*, 32; James Arthur Muller, and Jackson Kemper. "Two Letters from Bishop Kemper," *Historical Magazine of the Protestant Episcopal Church* 14, no. 4 (1945): 302–6.

that would, according to prelates like Doane and Kemper, lead to missionary successes. Christian brethren outside of the Episcopal Church "who have seemed to grow and multiply about us with a vigour so prolific," felt their lack of institutions and a durable tradition of worship. They knew "the want of those inherent principles of union which alone can bind in one large mass of mankind." Revivalistic sects and Evangelicals in the Old Northwest were "destitute of ancient landmarks," and consequently they strayed "insensibly from 'the old paths,' in which alone God's promise gives assurance of protection and of peace. Meanwhile, they turn instinctively to us. They recognize the doctrines which we hold, as the old faith which once was given to the Saints."[10]

If there were not ancient landmarks in the Old Northwest, Kemper would have to build them himself for future generations. The crown jewel of Kemper's ministry during his own lifetime, and his most enduring institutional legacy, was the founding of Nashotah House in southeast Wisconsin in 1842. Kemper wanted a serious seminary officially associated with the Episcopal Church as soon as he arrived in what remained a still-wild wilderness with limited white settlement. He was, he told a brother bishop, "more ready than ever to declare my thorough conviction that the establishment and future prosperity of our Church in the West greatly depends, in all human probability, upon the early organization of a school of the prophets in some part of this rapidly growing country." He wished "that several—not less than three and twelve would not be too many—of the students of the Theological Seminary should devote themselves to this sacred object." He chose a central location within his massive ecclesiastical territory, a spot, as he termed it, in the "interior of Wisconsin" that he believed had a "healthy" climate that would be congenial towards academic study. The cold weather was "scarcely as long and not more severe than in the Northern part of New York, while the atmosphere is said to be so dry during that season that it is quite congenial to consumptive patients." Access from all parts of the Old Northwest was a priority. Southeast Wisconsin, then still a US

[10] Doane, *The Missionary Bishop*, 13.

Territory, was "peculiarly accessible to the inhabitants of those states to which we must look for many years to come for the students who are to be prepared for the ministry of reconciliation. Extensive tracts of land could be purchased at government prices $1.25 per acre." Kemper was setting up a western analog to General Theological Seminary in New York City, but this new seminary would not be set in the urban bustle of a great American city. Kemper wanted an American Oxford in a bucolic setting. "The organization should be I think somewhat upon the plan of the Colleges of the English Universities." The village of Nashotah, which shared its name with the seminary Kemper created, was designed to be a churchly community where cloistered young men learned true churchmanship. Bishop Kemper wanted—and eventually got—"a limited number of fellows, bound together by certain rules, supplying their own vacancies, and being themselves a body corporate—devoted to the great object of preaching the Gospel and preparing young men for holy Orders." Anglican feeder institutions—Kemper proposed "grammar and collegiate schools"—would provide income and potential students. In keeping with the tradition of churchly universities in the United Kingdom, Kemper wanted to enforce celibacy "until a certain age or for a number of years should be required of most if not all the fellows for economy and study's sake, as we would constantly aim at making thorough and ripe scholars of the teachers as well as their pupils." A dispensation to marry could "be granted to an individual either by a unanimous vote or by resignation of his fellowship."[11]

  Classes at Nashotah began in 1841. It gained a more formal charter in 1845. From the outset, Nashotah House, as it was called in English fashion, gave its seminarians a thoroughly High Church reading of church history and theology. William Adams, James Lloyd Breck, and Rev. John Henry Hobart—the son of Bishop Hobart—formed the inaugural faculty. Kemper oversaw the seminary even as he undertook a series of episcopal visitations as far afield as northern Minnesota. Nashotah increasingly became the ministerial and geographic center of

[11] Stuckert, "Jackson Kemper, Presbyter," 130–51.

PART II: MISSIONARIES

Kemper's life and ministry. In 1846, he moved to a home near the seminary and lived there until his death. In 1847 he assumed the duties of provisional bishop of the diocese of Wisconsin. In 1854, he took up the mantle as ordinary bishop of Wisconsin. Outside of his vocal support for the defendant in the high profile trials of Bishop Onderdonk, Kemper's tenure went by quietly. In the Fall of 1869, Kemper experienced what was probably a stroke. He lingered through Christmas, and celebrated his eightieth birthday with his family. In April, 1870 he mustered enough strength to carry out a few duties, culminating in a series of confirmations. By the third week of May, 1870, exhaustion crippled him to the point he could not leave his bed. On May 21, 1870 Kemper slipped into a coma. He died quietly three days later.[12]

Kemper's legacy can still be seen in the halls of Nashotah House today. The seminary's High Church imprint profoundly influenced the direction of domestic missionary efforts in the United States. Evangelical churchmanship gave way to High Church commitments undeniably because of Nashotah's influence. Kemper's influence was more than merely churchly. Kemper, unlike prelates in the eastern states who enjoyed the comforts of bourgeois life in sizable cities, had to endure the same hardships that many of his parishioners did. Kemper did not come West and demand to be treated as a prince of the church. Instead he showed Episcopalians, and neighboring Lutherans and other religious groups what a working bishop looked like. Bishop Kemper did not democratize the Episcopal Church, but instead brought the Episcopal Church to the democratic frontier and created an enduring and uniquely American expression of High Church Anglicanism in what became the American Midwest.[13]

---

[12] *A Missionary Brotherhood in the Far West; or, The story of Nashotah, An Associate Mission and Theological Seminary* (London: Society for Promoting Christian Knowledge, 1873), 4-6; Jackson Kemper, "Bishop Jackson Kemper's Visit to Minnesota in 1843." *Minnesota History* 7, no. 3 (1926): 264–73; White, *An Apostle of the Western Church*, 228-229.

[13] Thomas C. Reeves, "James Lloyd Breck and the Founding of Nashotah House." *Anglican and Episcopal History* 65, no. 1 (1996): 50–81.

Philander Chase
1775-1852

Some men seem born to build. So we could say of Bishop Philander Chase. He spent most of his long ministry serving on the frontier of late 18th and early 19th century America. Out of the American forests he helped establish two dioceses and founded two institutions of higher learning. In so doing, he would work with tireless commitment to the Gospel and to Christ's Church. His determination would elicit praise but also, in one particular instance, frustration and opposition.

Philander Chase was born on December 14, 1775 in Cornish, New Hampshire. He was the fifteenth child and the youngest son of Dudley and Alice Chase. Dudley Chase served as a deacon in the local Congregational church. Laura Chase Smith, Philander's granddaughter, described her own great-grandparents as "born and bred in the Puritan faith."[1] In this faith Philander grew, worshipping with his parents and a large number of older siblings. He seemed to have by all accounts a loving home that provided for his physical, intellectual, and spiritual needs.

Some tensions did exist. Dudley held hopes that his youngest son would enter the ministry and took care for his schooling with that hope in mind. From Smith's account, young Philander did not share this desire but did not reject it out of the religious duty to honor one's father and mother. As had four brothers before him, a fifteen year-old Chase

---

[1] Laura Chase Smith, *The Life of Philander Chase* (New York: E.P. Dutton & Company, 1903), 31.

PART II: MISSIONARIES

enrolled at Dartmouth College in the Fall of 1791 with the possibility of vocational ministry in view.

During either his sophomore or junior year at Dartmouth, Chase found a copy of the Book of Common Prayer, which was not the most popular text in 1790s New England; the region was still in the shadow of the American Revolution and the Prayer Book's connection with the Church of England remained prevalent in so many minds. However, Chase's intellectual and even spiritual curiosity encouraged him to begin reading through it. He did not do so without guard or a willingness to critique. Later in life, Chase himself remembered that the Prayer Book "was examined and compared with the Word of God." The young man knew to test all things by God's infallible Scripture. By this examination and comparison, undertaken with others around him, "the more forcibly did its beauties strike their minds."[2] For Chase, the Prayer Book's use of and fidelity to God's Word formed the core of its loveliness as it formed the essence of its content. He would keep the connection between Scripture and the Prayer Book throughout the rest of his life, once entering a meeting of non-Episcopal Christians and declaring, "I hold in one hand a Bible, in the other a Prayer-book. The one teaches us how to live, and the other how to pray."[3]

Chase showed his evangelistic and missionary spirit immediately. He engaged his large family regarding its merits. Soon, most of his family and home neighborhood came to share Chase's love for Prayer Book worship and to concur with the particular tenets of the nascent Protestant Episcopal Church. Beyond the Prayer Book's conformity with God's Word and its beauty of style, the family also affirmed the Protestant Episcopal Church's "well-authenticated claims to an apostolic constitution in her ministry."[4]

Chase graduated from Dartmouth in the Summer of 1795. He now intended to enter Holy Orders within the Protestant Episcopal

---

[2] Philander Chase, *Bishop Chase's Reminiscences: An Autobiography*, 2nd Edition (Boston: James B. Dow, 1848), 1: 16.
[3] Smith, 261.
[4] *Ibid.*

Church. With that purpose, he traveled to Albany, NY where the Rev. Thomas Ellison, ordained in the Church of England, took Chase under his wing to prepare for Holy Orders. In 1796, he married Mary Fay of Hardwick, Massachusetts, then spent the next two years teaching students at a school in Albany while continuing his ordination studies.[5] Samuel Provoost, the first Bishop of New York, ordained Chase to the diaconate on May 10, 1798.[6] He later received ordination into the priesthood from the same bishop in November of 1799.

It is fitting that the classroom preceded Holy Orders for the young man. Chase's long ministry was defined by his work as an educator and as a missionary. Chase from the start saw the two roles as closely linked. Good educational institutions served the Church in its mission to proclaim the Gospel and add to the number of God's people.

After ordination as a deacon, Chase served as an itinerant missionary to the Northern and Western portions of the Diocese of New York. It is claimed that the first baptism he officiated was that of Ann Cooper Pomeroy, sister of Fenimore Cooper. As a deacon, he also preached regularly throughout the Diocese. The area he covered at the time consisted largely of the wilderness still untamed within the state of New York. Chase served this region with dogged intensity, traveling more than 4,000 miles in only 18 months.[7]

In the Autumn of 1799, shortly before being ordained to the presbyterate, he was asked to settle in as minister of two New York parishes, one in Fishkill, the other in Poughkeepsie.[8] Chase accepted, caring for those two congregations while also teaching in a local school to make ends meet financially. He would remain in that call for six years.

In 1805, New York's Coadjutor Bishop, Benjamin Moore, sent Chase to Louisiana where he would also minister for six years. The

---

[5] John N. Norton, *Life of Bishop Chase* (New York: General Protestant Episcopal School S. School Union, 1857), 18.
[6] Herman Griswold Batterson *A Sketchbook of the American Episcopate, 3rd Edition* (Philadelphia: J.P. Lippincott Company, 1891), 85.
[7] James Arthur Muller, "Philander Chase and the Frontier" in *Historical Magazine of the Protestant Episcopal Church* (14)(2)(June 1945): 169.
[8] Norton, 26-27.

PART II: MISSIONARIES

United States had acquired the territory from France only two years before in the Louisiana Purchase. Protestants in the area had sent out requests for clergy to come and minister there, given the dearth of Protestant influence and institutional structure from its longstanding possession by Roman Catholic France. Chase later claimed in his *Reminiscences* that he was "the first protestant minister that ever preached in Louisiana."[9] The priest would bring his wife with him on this mission but left his two young sons in the care of one of their uncles in Vermont. In Louisiana, Chase proved successful in establishing a parish for the Protestant Episcopal Church as well as a school for Protestant children of various denominations.

While in New Orleans, Chase purchased a slave. He later declared himself reticent to do so at the time but considered it necessary as the only means in a slave society to procure a quality servant. The slave escaped to England by boat after only three months. An elder Chase said the event troubled him at the time, but "mature reflections on the evils of slavery would heal the wound" and the slave's escape led to other great benefits to himself and to his parish.[10] Eleven years later, the slave was captured when returning to New Orleans. Chase, then in Ohio, refused to sell him to recoup the money he had lost but instead emancipated the man.[11] He later cared for two slaves, taken from a slave ship and brought to the Chase home in dire health. He and his family helped nurse one slave back to health. The other died and received burial by Chase. Of the latter he said "his soul was as precious in the eyes of his and our great Creator as that of anyone else."[12]

In 1811, he and his wife returned to the Northeast to reunite with their two children, now 14 and 13 years old. Here we see his commitment to the Prayer Book and its connection to Holy Scripture. He bemoaned that his sons had no Protestant Episcopal Church to attend while living

[9] *Reminisces*, 1: 55. See also James Thayer Addison, *The Episcopal Church in the United States, 1789-1931* (New York: Archon Books, 1969), 104.
[10] *Ibid.* I: 75.
[11] *Ibid.*, 1: 160.
[12] *Ibid.*, 1: 93. Chase's nephew was the abolitionist Salmon P. Chase, over whom the Bishop had significant influence on his education and upbringing.

in Vermont. This lack deprived them, "of the advantages which the Episcopal Church, in all her primitive ordinances, affords to the young" with "melancholy consequences." Chase then listed one advantage, that of "an Episcopal communion, which, by reading of the Holy Scriptures, rightly divided from the beginning of the year to the end thereof, might imbue the minds of the youth with heavenly knowledge."[13]

Upon returning, Chase served as rector of a parish in Hartford, Connecticut, from the Fall of 1811 until 1817. By his own later account, this time proved the most peaceful and happy in his ministry. He wrote of that period, "[i]t is to my remembrance as a dream of more than terrestrial delight."[14] He saw great growth in the parish and enjoyed the trappings and refinements of life on the East Coast.

In 1817, however, he resigned to take a role as "Missionary for the regions West of the Allegheny Mountains."[15] He sensed contrasting pulls, one being to continue in the sweet environs of Hartford. But he felt burdened for the West as well, to which so many men and women were moving and which sorely lacked clergy to minister to them. Chase had served on the frontier of Western New York before; now, he would take that missionary spirit to the new wilderness of Ohio. Though Ohio had joined the Union as a state in 1803, it remained sparsely populated (about 45,000 inhabitants) with much of its territory uncultivated. Churches and ministers were in short supply as well, especially for the Protestant Episcopal Church, which boasted a mere three clergy at the time of Chase's arrival.[16]

Chase made the long trek to Ohio, starting out on March 2 in three feet of snow, and immediately jumped into his missionary work. He preached his first sermon in the state on March 16th, 1817, in the city of Salem located southwest of Youngstown. Chase then traveled South, organizing parishes in central Ohio, including the recently-made state

[13] *Ibid.*, 1: 108.
[14] *Ibid.*, 1: 115.
[15] Batterson, 86.
[16] Muller, 171.

PART II: MISSIONARIES

capital of Columbus.[17] He next went to Cincinnati, where he held a meeting to form a parish there that was attended by future President William Henry Harrison.[18]

Chase then served as president of the state's first convention that met in Columbus on January 5, 1818, to form the Protestant Episcopal Church in Ohio. It was the first diocese formed outside of the original 13 states of the country.[19] A subsequent convention, held in Worthington in June, elected Chase as Ohio's first bishop. This momentous and joyous occasion was cut with personal tragedy, though. In May of 1818, Chase's wife passed away after suffering for well over a decade with tuberculosis.[20]

Chase's consecration took place on February 11, 1819 by presiding bishop William White of Pennsylvania with Bishop John Henry Hobart of New York, James Kemp of Maryland, and John Croes of New Jersey assisting.[21] Returning to Ohio, Chase faced a daunting task with a vast territory quickly growing in population but with so few clergy to minister Word and Sacrament according to the Prayer Book. As he had in New York, Chase worked tirelessly to build up parishes throughout the state. He reported in his autobiography that, between June 1820 and June of 1821, he preached 182 sermons, baptized 50 persons, and confirmed another 174.[22] In these efforts, he regularly traveled over a thousand miles in a year to pastor parishes across Ohio. He did so, too, without pay, as the diocese did not possess the funds to support his efforts.[23]

Chase did gain a new companion and partner in the ministry during this time. A year after his first wife's death, on July 4th, 1819, Chase married Sophia May Ingraham, whose family had lived in Boston, Philadelphia, and Greenvale, NY. She proved a diligent worker in

---

[17] Batterson, 86.
[18] Smith, 111-112.
[19] Muller, 173.
[20] Addison, 105. She was buried in Worthington, near Columbus, where the family had taken up residence.
[21] Smith, 137.
[22] Chase, 1: 177.
[23] Norton, 43-44.

God's vineyard as well, supporting her husband in his efforts wherever his ministry took him for decades to come.

In the Fall of 1821, Chase accepted a new educational role in addition to his episcopal work: the presidency of the College of Cincinnati,[24] today's University of Cincinnati. He did so, as he had other educational employment, in an effort to make financial ends meet (he by then had been granted some support as bishop but not sufficient to meet his and his family's needs). But Chase also worked in education again and again because he saw the necessity of learning for the good of the Church and its spread of the Gospel. In an 1819 address, he declared about the work of the church in founding educational institutions, "from these holy fountains have issued nearly all the streams of religious and moral science which now fertilized the Christian world."[25]

Ohio sorely needed more educational institutions, especially religious ones, in addition to more parishes. His concurrent goals of church planting and founding schools mixed together with particular intensity regarding the Western frontier, the people of which Chase always felt a special call to serve. Along these lines, Chase's most famous address came in, "A Plea for the West," published in 1827.[26] In that work, he pushed for others to support the cultivation of Christianity on the frontier. He noted how the quick settlement of the Ohio region had moved so fast that it had "far outstripped the means of religion and learning." Chase had seen the dissipation of religion and morality in the western parts of New York around the turn of the century due to the lack of churches as well as any religiously-centered education. He saw the same problem working in Ohio. He argued that his efforts sought to "remedy and prevent these dreadful evils, *ignorance* and *irreligion*."[27]

Both ignorance and irreligion needed remedied by establishing churches and schools. Establishing churches would spread the Gospel, thereby combating irreligion. On this score, in a sermon preached

---

[24] Prichard, 126.
[25] Chase, *Reminisces* 1: 172.
[26] Philander Chase, "A Plea for the West," (Boston: Samuel H. Parker, 1827).
[27] Chase, "A Plea," 3.

PART II: MISSIONARIES

in 1801, Chase implored that ministers should be sent throughout the American wilderness. Christian education would also remove ignorance about religion, about the ways of God in Himself and towards mankind.

Moreover, this dispelling of ignorance and irreligion would benefit society. Therefore, Chase regularly linked the truths of the Gospel to social and political goods, speaking about the benefits that message provided to, "the Church of Christ and to civil society."[28] In his "Plea for the West," Chase said the cause of founding a Christian seminary would "do something…for the common good"[29] as well as for the Church. In explanation, Chase declared that, "[h]uman society is like rich and fertile soil; it will seldom remain in a negative state. The weeds of error, of sin, and of bad habits, are sure to vegetate, where the salutary seeds of religion, morality, and good order, have not been sown and cultivated."[30]

At the suggestion of his son, Chase went to England to solicit funds for the Church in Ohio as well as for founding a theological college within the diocese. He became aware that an Eastern newspaper had reprinted portions of an English piece that lauded the growth of the Ohio Church, thus showing the possibility of obtaining financial assistance overseas.[31] Chase received opposition from other American bishops to the plan to create a theological educational institution. This opposition came especially from Bishop Hobart, who wanted all theological education in the Protestant Episcopal Church centered at the newer General Theological Seminary begun in his own Diocese of New York. An article also appeared in an English publication warning against Chase's mission, resulting in an initial cold response from those whom Chase contacted in England.[32] However, Chase worked tenaciously for eight months, raising $30,000 from subscribers across Great Britain. There, he received the help of the second Lord Kenyon and Lord Gambier, who opened doors to others throughout England. In his

[28] Chase, *Reminiscences*, I: 40.
[29] Chase, "A Plea," 3.
[30] Chase, *Reminiscences*, I: 38.
[31] Addison, 105.
[32] Norton, 46.

pitch, Chase played up his diocese's humble status, referring to himself as the "backwoods bishop."[33]

Ohio's legislature incorporated a school in December of 1824, an institution which would become Kenyon College. In addition to his other work, Chase served as Kenyon's president. These early years showed much promise but also saw many challenges, including continued construction of needed campus buildings. During this time, Chase kept a close eye and a tight grip on all that went on at the school. This control soon wore on those serving under the bishop. In 1831, faculty at Kenyon presented a formal accusation against Chase for ruling the institution with "absolute and unlimited power." The subsequent state episcopal convention, begun on September 7th, unanimously adopted a report calling for a board of trustees to be formed for the College, which then should draft clear rules delineating the duties, powers, and rights of all persons at the college, including the bishop in his capacity serving as the institution's president.

Chase chaffed at the correction and promptly resigned on September 9, 1831, both as bishop and for all positions related to Kenyon. He believed the Convention's move contradicted the wishes of those who had donated to form Kenyon and misunderstood its nature as an institutional arm of the Church. His resignation produced shock among those attending the Convention. Attempts to dissuade Bishop Chase from his action proved unavailing and the body eventually accepted his resignation.[34] Removal from the school and the diocese was painful for Chase and his family. But Chase's bishopric had born great success. At the time of his resignation, forty-three parishes had been organized in Ohio with nineteen clergy—a significant increase from the time of his arrival and consecration.[35]

[33] Muller, 174.
[34] Norton, 70. Smith gives a slight hint of shared criticism here, rare for her biography of her grandfather, saying, "after all, when the facts of the whole proceedings are looked squarely in the face, and when it is considered what they meant, one can but regret that more time had not been taken before the great decision was made." See Smith, 238.
[35] Muller, 176.

PART II: MISSIONARIES

In the Spring of 1832, Chase bought a farm in Branch County, Michigan, which borders the state of Indiana. He spent three years building and tending that farm. He interacted with local Native Americans and fought off the many wolves who still lurked in the area. Chase also held services in his home and other nearby locations, including South Bend, Indiana, bringing with him a basket filled with Prayer Books, explaining to those unfamiliar the rhythms and intentions of its worship.[36]

Yet his work would not end in Southern Michigan. In 1835, Chase received and accepted a call to serve as the bishop of the newly formed Diocese of Illinois. He again found himself serving a diocese in the wilderness with little structure and no funding. Only one Episcopal Church building existed in the state with only four presbyters and two deacons to serve the flock.[37] He again had no salary from the diocese. Undeterred, the Bishop threw himself into this situation with the same gusto he had exhibited when beginning his work in Ohio nearly twenty years before.

Chase traveled far and wide across the 55,000 square miles of the new diocese. He again went to England to raise funds for it, collecting $10,000 by Spring of 1836.[38] Repeating his work from Ohio, Bishop Chase formed a new college, called Jubilee, in 1839.[39] He continued to travel, raising funds for that institution for the rest of his life, including making his appeal across large swaths of the United States. Unlike Kenyon College, which grew into a well-established institution, Jubilee never found its financial footing and closed in the 1860s. Still, its founding and early maintenance again showed Chase's amazing skill and determination to provide godly education to those on the American frontier.

---

[36] Smith, 256-257.
[37] Muller, 178; Smith, 264.
[38] Addison, 109.
[39] Charles Comfort Tiffany, *A History of the Protestant Episcopal Church in the United States of America*, 2nd Edition (Charles Scribner's Sons, 1895), 437.

Chase's diocese continued to grow, as did the state of Illinois, to which droves of settlers moved during these years. By 1846, the four to five parishes with which Chase had begun grew to thirty while the six original clergy ballooned to nineteen.[40] In this diocese, Chase would serve to the end of his earthly days. During this time, Chase also rose to the position of the Presiding Bishop of the Protestant Episcopal Church, a position held by the longest-serving bishop within that Church. Chase sat from February 15, 1843, until his death nearly a decade later.

During his time as Presiding Bishop, the Protestant Episcopal Church continued to face liturgical and doctrinal pressures, especially related to the rise in England of the Oxford Movement and its growing influence across the ocean. Theologically, Chase rejected these efforts, affirming the inherently Protestant character of the Episcopal Church. During the first national convention in which he was Presiding Bishop, the Convention published a pastoral letter which strongly critiqued elements of that movement. In particular, the letter opposed what it saw as Oxford's undermining of the Protestant distinctives of the Church of England and Her daughter churches, thereby attempting to move these bodies in the direction of Roman Catholicism. This letter affirmed that salvation is by faith alone, through grace alone, in Christ alone: that "[n]othing is more characteristic of our church than these Scriptural truths."[41] This connection to Scripture continued Chase's long standing connection of the Prayer Book in particular and the Episcopal Church in general to the preeminent authority of Scripture. From his Dartmouth days on, he had dedicated himself to the spread of Prayer Book worship and Biblical fidelity. For from the first time he found the Prayer Book, he loved it for its beauty. But most essentially, he loved it, he found it beautiful as a liturgy faithful to Holy Scripture. The Prayer Book complemented and supported the Bible in his view, seeing the

---

[40] Norton, 94.
[41] Philander Chase, *Pastoral Letters from the House of Bishops to the Clergy and Members of the Protestant Episcopal Church* (Philadelphia: Edward C. Biddle, 1845), 261.

entire tradition of the Protestant Episcopal Church as grounded in God's Word.

Moreover, the letter explicitly contrasted the Protestant Episcopal Church's doctrine from "the Romish communion." It minced no words in contrasting itself to Rome, condemning "the *blasphemous* doctrine of *transubstantiation,* and the abominable idolatries of the mass."[42] In clear response to John Henry Newman's Tract 90, the letter went on to say that, "The articles of our church afford us stable ground on which to stand in guarding you from these errors of the Church of Rome. Take these articles in the sense of their framers and as set forth and investigated by the most distinguished divines, and there can be no mistake. These articles thus interpreted, we hold in great reverence, and entreat you to consider them in the same light, listening to no interpretation that will draw you from the Protestant faith."[43]

Chase's death came on September 20, 1852, with the Bishop having reached the age of 76. Bishop Chase left behind an impressive legacy, one driven by a missionary zeal that took him again and again into the American wilderness to found churches where none existed. In this spirit, he helped to start two dioceses: Ohio and Illinois. Chase also held a life-long commitment to education. He founded two colleges, one which has endured even if it has lost its original focus on training clergy and its orthodoxy in theological matters.

Chase's legacy lives on in the dioceses he helped shepherd and the remaining educational institution he founded. God blessed his missionary zeal. He spread love for Scripture and for Prayer Book worship throughout the American frontier. His is a spirit which our own time, our own Church, needs anew.

---

[42] *Ibid.,* 264.
[43] *Ibid.,* 265.

James Hervey Otey
1800-1863

Nineteenth century Protestant presumptions about the relationship between Christianity and education relied on a division that was churchly and secular, not on a paradigm that divided the secular and the religious. This distinction was vital because it was a taxonomy that allowed Protestants in the Episcopal Church to fully support constitutional disestablishment while simultaneously arguing that religious education was a benefit to Christian *and* secular America. James Hervey Otey, first Episcopal bishop of Tennessee, championed the importance of Christian education for society throughout his prelacy and proved one of the most important creators of Episcopal education in the South. Best known for founding the Episcopal college at Sewanee, Otey established schools at parishes across Tennessee and the South.

Bishop Otey pushed the national Episcopal Church to prioritize education and particularly Christian education. At the church's General Convention in 1859, he used his sermon—later published as *Christian Education*—to emphasize the societal benefits of the education provided through the Episcopal Church. Few other topics, argued Otey, could "more fitly claim the serious consideration of a Christian assembly, or the anxious reflections of American citizens, or the deep and pious thoughts of the right reverend fathers, ministers and brethren composing this council of the church" than the importance of Christian education. "This is not a subject, which may or ought to awaken interest, only in the bosoms of Christian parents. Its range is wide enough

PART II: MISSIONARIES

to embrace all the families of the land." Christian education's influence extended "to many other interests than those merely of domestic life. It is the boast of our countrymen, that their social well-being is not dependent for its source nor for its continuance on the circumstances which may surround an individual." Just because someone was not religious did not mean they shouldn't receive a Christian education. Otey, more than any other Episcopal churchman in the South, made Christian-influenced education a reality for those who otherwise might not have had one.[1]

A light dusting of snow, coupled with ample sunshine, greeted the local gentry of Bedford County, Virginia as they made their way to church on the first Sunday of the new year and new century. 1800 found Virginia near the height of its cultural, political, and social influence in the still very young American republic. Sunday, January 5, found Elizabeth Matthews Otey and her husband Major Isaac Otey less mobile than they normally were. The local Episcopal parish lay some miles distant. The Oteys did not attend church regularly, and Elizabeth's age—she was almost thirty-five—and Bedford's relative isolation made the already precarious prospect of pregnancy even more tenuous. This pregnancy was the twelfth that Elizabeth carried to full term. On 27 January, 1800, she delivered a healthy baby boy. Isaac and his wife named their son James Hervey. The infant took his middle name from a popular British writer of the era. The scant details of the future bishop's boyhood indicate a conventional childhood blessed by James enjoying good health in an era when children routinely faced fatal illnesses. His parents enjoyed enough means to send him to a local academy. Eventually he attended a more formal school in New London, the market town of Bedford County. Otey enjoyed learning, and read voraciously. He did not emerge as an adolescent paragon of spiritualist piety. Like many boys in his era, his reading interests tended towards the great men and

---

[1] James Hervey Otey, *Christian Education: A Sermon Before the General Convention of the Protestant Episcopal Church United States of America at Saint Paul's Church the city of Richmond on Wednesday, October 5, 1859* (Richmond, VA: Enquirer Book and Job Office, 1859), 5-7

great battles playing themselves out on the battlefields of Europe. Otey's friend and future brother bishop William Mercer Green wrote of the former's education in the foothills of the Blue Ridge that the instruction Otey received, while "not extensive in its range, was thorough in its character." Otey "early evinced a studious and inquiring disposition, being an eager and attentive listener to the simple and honest counsels of his father, and sharing with him in the popular discussions of the day." In the second decade of the nineteenth century "the wars of Napoleon were the current topics of the village schoolboy, as well as of the minister in his cabinet. The boy's young mind was fired with ambitious views of distinction, but without any definite aim." In Otey's "enthusiastic imagination, Napoleon was the embodiment of his highest conceptions of human greatness; and, doubtless, formed in him an unconscious resolve to win for himself some one or other of the prizes of life."

Isaac Otey saw his son's intellectual potential, and according to William Green the elder Otey made meaningful financial sacrifices to further his son's education. James Otey gained admittance to the University of North Carolina, the South's premier state college. Otey loved learning, and the faculty at Chapel Hill fired his passion for education. Otey grew particularly close to Elisha Mitchell, the college's professor of mathematics and one of the chief explorers of the Appalachian Mountains in North Carolina. Mitchell died tragically in 1858 surveying the peak in the Black Mountains—the highest point in eastern North America—that eventually bore his name. In a eulogy delivered just after Mitchell's interment on Mt Mitchell, Otey thanked his professor for upholding Christianity in the state university's educational regime against complaints by secularists and sectarians who "would see every institution of learning in the land crumbled into ruins rather than not have a direct share in its management and government." Mitchell believed Christianity had a place in the curriculum without needing ecclesiastical oversight. Otey recalled that Mitchell infused "the religious element, as much as possible, into his instructions in the lecture room, and more especially in his conversation with those who were so fortunate as to win his personal regard." Otey reminisced about his time as "an untaught, undisciplined and unsophisticated youth," and pondered "what a deep impression" Mitchell's "commanding form, his noble brow on which mind seemed enthroned, and his dark, lustrous eye made upon our young hearts."[2]

There were no colleges and few primary schools to speak of, and churches were generally peopled by irregular attendees and itinerant ministers of varying levels of education. After his education at the University of North Carolina at Chapel Hill he moved to Franklin, Tennessee. In Franklin he began what was to be a lifelong commitment to education. He opened a school for boys and taught what could be called a classical curriculum there for a year. In that same year he married Eliza Pannill, originally from Petersburg, Virginia.[3]

Accounts differ as to when exactly Otey began the spiritual journey that eventually led to him sitting in Tennessee's episcopal chair. In one account, Otey first encountered the prayer book when as a tutor at the University North Carolina he—still largely irreligious—was charged with leading the college's chapel services. A colleague was said to have loaned Otey a prayer book, thus introducing him to Anglican churchmanship. In another account, the newly married Otey began a friendship with a local man in Tennessee in 1822 that led the latter to give Otey a copy of the Book of Common Prayer, the first one it seems that the latter had ever owned. It is also possible that both accounts are true. The details of Otey's reception into the Episcopal Church are not known. Otey never embraced, personalized, or expounded overly emotional articulations of his faith, but that did not mean he became a ritualist. He described himself as a "prayer book churchman," and it was in the Book of Common Prayer that he found a meaningful Anglican identity. By 1822 Otey's relationship with the prayer book was such that it led him to make significant changes in his own life while his career as

---

[2] James H. Otey and David L. Swain, *A Memoir of the Rev. Elisha Mitchell D.D.* (Chapel Hill, NC: J.M. Henderson, 1858), 67-68.

[3] E. Clowes Chorley, "How Our Church Came to Tennessee," in Hugh L. Burleson ed., *How Our Church Came to Our Country* (Milwaukee, WI: Morehouse Publishing Co., 1920), 81.

an educator was in its infancy. Otey enjoyed a good reputation with his neighbors, and his eventual return to Tennessee as bishop can be seen as evidence of time well spent even before he was a member of the Episcopal Church. He was an imposing man, over six feet four inches tall with jet black hair. Local Tennesseans called him Cherokee, a term of endearment and respect in a place that saw the fighting prowess of local indigenous peoples as worthy of respect, even in an era of widespread anti-native racism.[4]

Otey was reluctant to give details about the spiritual transformation he underwent in Tennessee. Whatever the "hound of heaven" did in Tennessee, it was such that Otey decided to move back to North Carolina and seek employment while he reconciled himself to joining the Episcopal Church. In Warrenton, North Carolina—along the state's northeastern border with Virginia—he set up a Latin school for local boys, most of whom hailed from what passed for the area's local gentry. (His students included the less than aristocratic brothers Braxton and Thomas Bragg, who would figure prominently in the fortunes of the Confederacy during the American Civil War.) Otey's own religious formation had been neglected, despite his attendance at the University of North Carolina. Unlike his contemporary Bishop William Meade in Virginia, Otey himself was reticent about writing on personal matters throughout his ministry. What we do know is that he contacted William Mercer Green, an instructor at the University of North Carolina and an Episcopal priest, and asked to be baptized. Green obliged, and shortly thereafter, North Carolina's bishop John Stark Ravenscroft confirmed Otey into the Episcopal Church. Otey taught for two more years. While he taught, Otey also became a postulate in the diocese of North Carolina. In 1825, Bishop Ravenscroft ordained Otey as a deacon. Two years later he became a presbyter.[5]

[4] Moultrie Guerry, "Makers of Sewanee: I. James Hervey Otey." *The Sewanee Review* 40, no. 4 (1932): 396–403.
[5] Bishop Thomas Frank Gailor, "James Hervey Otey—First Bishop of Tennessee." *Historical Magazine of the Protestant Episcopal Church* 4, no. 1 (1935): 53–56; Grady McWhiney, *Braxton Bragg and Confederate Defeat*. Vol. 1. (New York: Columbia University Press, 1969), 1-9; Samuel S. Hill and

PART II: MISSIONARIES

Although he began his career as a cleric in North Carolina, Tennessee called Otey and he moved back to Middle Tennessee. Although no longer an uninhabited wilderness, Tennessee still retained the rougher aspects of frontier life. Otey never claimed to be an intellectual, and the gifts he brought to the church in Tennessee proved to be more social than scholarly. For the Episcopal church to be taken seriously, it would need actual churches, and for local parishes to be taken seriously, they needed to be staffed by priests who could command the respect, if not affection, of the local populations. Otey's prioritization of education, particularly for adolescent boys in frontier Tennessee, was based in his commitment to civilizing the frontier, but Otey also maintained a deeply churchly, and not merely civilizational, commitment to Christianity. Otey was "impressed by the need not only for 'reading, writing, and arithmetic' but for good sound religious and moral training." Otey and many other orthodox churchmen believed that the frontier was in particular need of moral and religious training, but not every priest was to endure the social and moral realities of Middle Tennessee. Otey's stature certainly helped him. On one occasion when he had to spend the night in a hotel room, an infamous local gambler came into the room and told Otey to get out. The gambler, accustomed to successfully intimidating the local clientele, threatened to throw the priest out of the room if he didn't leave. Otey rose to his full height and told the gambler to feel his arm muscles before he tried to forcefully remove Otey. The gambler left the room, and Otey went back to sleep. [6]

Life as the only Episcopal priest in Tennessee meant that Otey served as a bi-vocational minister. He taught and also tried to organize an Episcopal parish in the environs of Franklin, Tennessee. He succeeded and held the first organized Episcopal services in Franklin's Masonic lodge. Unlike Early Republic Presbyterians who debated the appropriateness of ministers also being Masons, High Churchmen in the Episcopal Church never saw membership in secret societies as

Charles Lippy eds., *Encyclopedia of Religion in the South* (Macon, GA: Mercer University Press, 2005), 575.
[6] Guerry, "Makers of Sewanee: I. James Hervey Otey", 396-403.

incompatible with good churchmanship, and Otey remained a member of a Masonic lodge after his ordination. He also "attained its highest degree." William Mercer Green argued that Otey admired the beauty of its ritual and the purity of its precepts, but regarded the whole system as a mere reflection of the brighter sunlight of the Gospel." Otey justified his presence in the lodge claiming that the presence of active Christians "adorned their well-deserved honors" of Masonic observances "with the higher distinction of a Christian life."

Attraction to ritual increasingly defined Episcopal churchmen in the 1830s and 1840s. The Tractarian movement's inception in Great Britain eventually led to American bishops and presbyters embracing High Church innovation. High Churchmanship in the nineteenth century, however, did not preclude a simultaneous identification with Evangelicals in the Episcopal Church. Green described Otey as a churchman who had both High Church and evangelical proclivities. Ravenscroft "imbued" in Otey "a belief in the Church as the Representative Body of Christ: One in its Divine organization, Holy in character, Catholic in extent, and Apostolic in its Ministry." Otey affirmed the traditional Anglican understanding of apostolic succession and "was fully convinced of the unbroken succession in our Episcopate; he looked upon schism as a sin, and both inculcated and practised a rigid conformity to Rubrical and Canonical Order." "Nothing," noted Bishop Green "more than this would seem necessary to place him in the category of what is known as 'High Churchmen.'" But, "on the other hand, his yet earlier youthful associations had inclined him to look with equal approval upon the Church and the surrounding denominations, and to concede to all claimants alike the right to minister in holy things." Otey stood between "these two extremes of Church thought," and it was between the High Churchmen and the Evangelicals that "his true position might have been found." As a presbyter and later as bishop Otey "was consequently the object of attack by the zealots of both parties, but more especially of the latter [High Church party]." Otey's "unceremonious ejection of the crosses and candlesticks at Riverside ought certainly to exonerate him from the suspicion of being a High Church Ritualist; and his equally ungracious treatment of certain publications of the 'Evangelical Knowledge Society' should as surely acquit him of favoring the levelling and disintegrating views of that association." Green praised the "marked characteristic of Bishop Otey's mind" that allowed him to "look away from party influence in judging of all matters affecting in any way the nature or welfare of the Church." [7]

The specific type of syncretic High Churchmanship practiced by Otey, his mentor Ravenscroft, and to a lesser extent William Mercer Green stemmed less from a systematic understanding of Anglican theology and more from a belief that the democratization of American religion had bred religious disorder dangerous to the souls of Americans and their society. Otey embraced some but not all aspects of the Tractarian movement because he believed the church needed to return to historical order in order to survive in what many churchmen believed was a religious anarchy that would eventually threaten society at large. In an 1838 address to the Episcopal Church's mission board, Otey laid out his understanding of the essential weaknesses of the American socio-religious order. "Never since the world began, we may safely say, has there been furnished such a theatre for the dissemination of truth or of error, as is presented in the actual condition of the American people." The bishop warned that "every man among us can gain some influence, and through the tremendous power of the press, speaking with its thousand tongues, can propagate his opinions, and spread them, in a few days, from the lakes of Canada to the Gulf of Mexico; from the shores of the Atlantic, to the base of the Rocky Mountains." He praised republican institutions for ensuring "freedom and protection to men of all nations, and offer a guarantee of safety to all, in the entertainment and diffusion of every shade of religious belief." Nonetheless, he feared that there were "men standing upon our own coasts, the determined and uncompromising enemies of the cross, with hands stretched out and inviting those who fraternize with them, to come and aid them in the unholy cause of opposition to piety, virtue and religion." Anti-Christian agitators

[7] Green, *Memoir of Rt. Rev. James Hervey Otey*, 120

"would, under the pretence of making men free, demolish the fair fabric of our civil and religious freedom; lay in ruins its beautiful proportions by removing every restraint to unbridled licentiousness, and triumph in the prevalence of anarchy, impiety and crime."[8]

Fears over the potential rise of anti-Christian social norms led Otey to worry particularly about the morality and piety of the young. "The education of youth" remained a priority for his ministry, and he "endeavored to awaken and keep alive an interest in the establishment of both male and female schools." The diocese of Tennessee, "when he first entered it, was the abode of the pioneer and the hardy backwoodsman, who looked with contempt upon learning and refinement, especially in connection with the ministry of the Gospel." Anglican services "were something so strange to them, that the Bishop would afterwards illustrate it by telling what one of these rude sons of the forest was once heard to say to another: 'Come, let us go and hear that man preach, and his wife jaw back at him,' alluding to the responses made by Mrs. Otey, who was oftentimes the only respondent in the congregation." It was not surprising then that "the Church in Tennessee was a 'little one' indeed, when Mr. Otey determined to make that State the field of his lifelong labors." There was only one Anglican presbyter "within its wide borders; viz., Rev. John Davis (Deacon), who had been sent there by a Missionary Society at the North, and was feebly laboring amidst a world of obstacles." Otey needed help " if the Church was ever to have a name and be a power in accomplishing the work so much needed in this portion of the Lord's vineyard." Otey recruited presbyters as best he could, and he generally looked to North Carolina, largely because that state's Anglican leadership tended to mirror the old High Churchmanship that Otey so admired in his mentor John Stark Ravenscroft.

Unlike most other Early Republic prelates, Otey journeyed to Europe during his episcopacy. Observers in Nashville considered Otey's 1851 trip a momentous occasion in the state's life. Local newspapers kept

[8] James Hervey Otey, *The Triennial Sermon Before the Bishops, Clergy, and Laity Constituting the Board of Missions of the Protestant Episcopal Church in the United States*, 13

track of his progress and his traveling companions. Otey's choice of traveling companions gives some information regarding his views on politics and society in the antebellum era. He traveled mainly with Edwin H. Ewing, a former Whig congressman from a noted Middle Tennessee family. Otey took the trip for the purpose of leisure. By the Spring of 1851 he had been doing the hectic work of a bishop for nearly two decades. Although Otey was a relatively healthy man of what passed for a robust physical constitution in the middle of the nineteenth century, the labor of the episcopacy wore on him. Europe proved to be a welcome respite.[9]

While leisure and rest were the public reasons Otey offered for his trip, he also ensured his itinerary took him through the major college towns of Great Britain and Western Europe. Otey's interest in education became more intense in the 1850s and much of his energy turned towards creating a more authentically Anglican college or university in the South. Church politics and the great liturgical and theological controversies continued to upset the stability of the Church of England in the 1850s. More ritualistic interpretations of the prayer book made High Churchmen appear broadly sympathetic to Tractarians in the United States, and in Great Britain High Churchmen reinforced their Protestant commitments by offering support to the more broad church hierarchy of the Church of England. In particular, Otey joined with the famously High Church bishop of Oxford, Samuel Wilberforce, in the latter's vehement protest of parliament over that body's perceived lax response to Pope Pius IX's reestablishment of the Roman Catholic hierarchy in Great Britain. Parliament responded to Pius by ordering any Roman Catholic who used the title of bishop to pay a fine of one hundred pounds. Wilberforce, along with prominent evangelical and High Church bishops, saw the parliamentary response as outrageously permissive. Otey wrote to Wilberforce that he fully concurred with the Church of England's response to what was widely perceived as a Roman

---

[9] *The Tennessean* (Nashville, TN), 24 April 1851.

assault on the church, backed by Whig politicians and nonconformist religious leaders like young Charles Spurgeon. [10]

The innate conservatism and even traditionalism of Otey revealed itself in letters about industrialization in Great Britain. Even Tennessee embraced capitalism and some aspects of industrialism, particularly under Whig governor Neil Brown. Governor Brown saw much to admire about the antebellum North and argued that if "the same spirit of internal improvement and education" were applied to Tennessee the latter would become "the first state in the Union and the world." Far from being a paragon of agrarian traditionalism, southern states—particularly Georgia and Tennessee—urbanized rapidly in the years that preceded the Civil War. Otey's experience in Britain made him less than enthusiastic about industrialization than other Whigs in the North and South. "Tower like chimneys" he lamented, belched out "dark volumes of smoke…beclouding the atmosphere as far as the eye could reach." Industrial contributions to society, he feared, were not enough to offset the essential fact that factories "darken the land & shroud the heavens in gloom." In other journal entries Otey blamed industry for sickness and a generally unhealthy society. Otey's Whig sympathies hinged much more on the necessity of maintaining Christian moral precepts and conserving traditional morality than with finance or industry. [11]

Economic and societal change and the quixotic nature of humans in general formed the chief reason why Otey believed Christian education needed to be given to American children. Christianity alone offered a metaphysic enduring enough to withstand societal change. "Many of us" he told his fellow bishops, "will probably live to see the sceptre of our civil condition transferred, and the destinies of this nation, social

[10] Edwin T. Greninger ed., *Otey's Journal: being the account by James Hervey Otey, A.B., M.A., D.D., L.L.D., first bishop of the Tennessee Diocese of the Protestant Episcopal Church, of his travels in the summer of 1851 in England, Scotland, Ireland, and Wales* (The Overmountain Press, 1994), 8-10.

[11] John Ashworth, *Slavery, Capitalism, and Politics in the Antebellum Republic: Volume 1: Commerce and Compromise, 1820-1850* (Cambridge and London: Cambridge University Press, 1995), 483; James Hervey Otey, *Otey's Journal*, 25.

and religious, intellectual and moral, public and individual, pass into the hands of the little beings whose minds are now occupied with the toys of childhood." There was, however, no guarantee that the present generation of children would be virtuous republicans as adults. "The next race of the sovereign people may be as degenerate as the successor of an absolute monarch." History in the form of the Roman Republic and the French Revolution offered a warning to Americans on the inherently unstable nature of republican societies.

> The voice of history proclaims the grave and impressive lesson, that the glories of republics have been evanescent—that their energies have become effete and languid, in the transmission through fewer generations than those of some hereditary dynasties. They seem to resemble those vegetable productions which bloom more magnificently, and bear a richer fruitage, but arrive at earlier decay and decrepitude. How shall we, on whom the care of ours is now incumbent, maintain the vital principle with undiminished healthfulness and vigor, that it may flourish for us, and for those who follow after us? There is but one method, and that method is obvious; it is easy, and it is secure, if faithfully pursued.

"Here," Otey reminded the bishops, "within our reach, under our almost unlimited control, and in a ductile state, is the very material on whose shape the stability of our institutions must depend."[12]

Schooling, under largely Protestant control, was the material that gave institutions stability through Christian philosophy and religious principles. "The alternative is before us either to leave that material to be moulded by external circumstances highly unfavorable, or to give it form by that plastic touch of education, whose moral impress the droppings of time can never efface, nor any stroke of accident destroy." He quoted the aphorism that "the child is father to the man." Foundations

---

[12] Otey, *Christian Education*, 6.

of character and destiny "of every individual element of that rational multitude whose mind will sway the world of thirty years hence, will be laid permanently and indestructibly before it has attained the twelfth year of its being." By the time a child became a teenager, they would either be educated as a Christian, or they would be educated as something else. "Subsequent influences," he warned, might "strengthen or impair" the foundation of Christian education offered, "but they never can displace it." Bishop Otey rejected the notion that "the characters of men" resulted "from their own investigations: the patterns are not selected and approved by a mature judgment: they are formed by the combined development of those associations and sympathies of childhood, from whose abiding influence no reasonings or efforts of mature years will ever entirely emancipate them." The choice for the Episcopal Church was clear, warned Otey. "You must communicate, or you must withhold from that wave of human society which follows after you, and will soon rise in your place, those principles whose infusion will make it pure, and whose absence will cause it to spread bitterness, corruption and desolation wherever it rolls."

The belief that God could be taken out of education worried Otey. Such presumptions, warned Otey, were "prevalent and dangerous." Unless this anti-religious trend was "very soon checked, this nation will in a few years be made lamentably, mournfully and woefully sensible." Dechristianized education was, Otey noted, "advocated sometimes explicitly and often impliedly by men who are set as watchmen for the defence of society from the incursions of moral and religious evil; and yet it virtually admits the claims of infidelity." These assumptions were "precisely the principle which was preached by skeptics of the last century, and was in truth the fruitful parent of that direful progeny of evils which the world witnessed in the excesses and horrors of the French revolution."[13]

It was Otey's belief that conservative churchmanship and churchly education inevitably led to the maintenance of a healthy Christian

---

[13] *Ibid.*, 12

PART II: MISSIONARIES

social order that led him to spearhead the founding of the University of the South at Sewanee. The college was the first major Episcopal church college founded in nearly two decades, and the first of its type in the Trans-Appalachian South or the Deep South. The college would undoubtedly become Otey's greatest legacy. Only a few years after the founding of Sewanee, the vehemently unionist bishop died, his spirit and health broken from supporting the Union cause in Tennessee as the secession winter and spring of 1861 tore the Union in two. Otey's legacy, however, was not soon forgotten. In August 1879, bishop William Mercer Green addressed the gathered trustees of the University of the South. Sewanee, then only two decades old, nonetheless had become a leading institution of higher learning. Although the university owed its charter to the famed fighting bishop of Louisiana, Leonidas Polk, it was more properly the brainchild of Bishop Otey. [14]

Otey influenced Green and other southern Episcopalians and preceded the latter as a missionary bishop in Mississippi. Otey, Green, and Polk remained painfully aware that the Episcopal Church was increasingly overshadowed socially by the growing Evangelical movements of the era. By the 1830s, the second generation of Evangelicals—Baptists, Disciples of Christ, and Methodists—achieved a measure of respectability their revivalist predecessors could only envy. The success of Evangelical laypeople fed the respectability of popular Evangelical ministers who drew sizable numbers of congregants through dynamic preaching. This symbiotic relationship eventually, argued Nathan Hatch, sapped the revivalist fervor and what he called the populism of southern Evangelicals. A new class of self-consciously elite Evangelicals directed their efforts at building colleges, but their churches never again experienced the degree or type of sociological growth they enjoyed during the first four decades of the Nineteenth Century. [15]

---

[14] George R. Fairbanks, *History of the University of the South, at Sewanee, Tennessee* (Jacksonville, FL: H. & W.B. Drew Co., 1905), 1.

[15] Nathan O. Hatch, *The Democratization of American Christianity* (New Haven and London: Yale University Press 1989), 195.

Episcopalians remained circumspect about Evangelical religiosity. The less-institutional nature of Evangelical religion did not, they noted, create the type of educational milieu that educated young Episcopalians in their faith. Evangelical colleges were seen as insufficient. When Episcopalians passed "from under the parental eye" in preparatory schools they did not have "institution fairly within our reach" where confirmed Episcopalians could be "kept under the influence of those Christian principles" and churchly instruction "to which we pledged them in baptism, which we have accepted and hold as of the essence of Christ's religion, which we would transmit in their vigor to them and through them, unmarred, to our latest posterity." Evangelical education was not appropriate for southern Episcopalians. The most tolerable institution for most southern Episcopalians to send their children remained the College of New Jersey in Princeton, but that was far away and in a free state. What was needed was truly churchly education, safely overseen by the hierarchy of the Protestant Episcopal Church and not given to the populist dispositions of Evangelical religion.[16]

Otey believed that the Evangelical South had not created a true religious society or churchly religious practice. Bishop Green noted that Otey "saw that religious culture was the great want of the people of the South-West." Otey was convinced that knowledge "of the Church in its Catechisms and Creeds, and its life giving sacraments, should be taught side by side with the usual branches of both an elementary and a higher education." It was Otey who first called "the attention of our South-Western Churchmen to the necessity of establishing such a University as this." The efforts of Otey and the founding of Sewanee represent an opportunity to rethink scholarship that privileges and over-prioritizes democratization and liberalization as hallmarks of Protestant education in the Early Republic. Sewanee was not illiberal, but it was fundamentally traditional in a time and place where Nathan Hatch

---

[16] Fairbanks, *History of the University of the South*, 12-13.

argued culture, religious culture included, mounted a frontal assault on tradition, mediating elites, and institutions. [17]

---

[17] William Mercer Green, *Address Delivered Before the Board of Trustees, August 4, 1879* (Charleston, SC: Walker, Evans, and Cogswell, 1879), 12; Hatch, *The Democratization of American Christianity*, 182.

Part III

Intellectuals

John Stark Ravenscroft
1772-1830

In the summer of 1824 John Stark Ravenscroft sat down at his desk at the rectory of Christ Church parish in Raleigh, NC and wrote a letter to a congregation 125 miles southwest. A group of Episcopalians in Mecklenburg County had gathered enough financial support to begin the construction of an Episcopal parish in the largely Presbyterian county that bordered South Carolina. Ravenscroft crafted a pastoral letter that at once encouraged the newly constituted congregation of Saint James parish and admonished them to keep the true Catholic and Apostolic faith. Christians and particularly Protestants in the United States in the early Republic, Ravenscroft feared, no longer understood rightly the doctrine of the church. "By the doctrine of the Church, I mean that article of our public creed, in which we profess our belief in the Holy Catholic Church-or, as it is more definitely expressed, in the Nicene Creed, in one 'Catholic and Apostolick Church.'" Ravenscroft was a High Churchman but he assured his flock that they needed to understand "the meaning" of the words Catholic and Apostolic. "For such is the ignorance which is fast spreading over us, on this and similar subjects, that many, when they hear us express our belief in the Holy Catholic Church, associate us with the Church of Rome." Associating the terms catholic and apostolic with the Roman church often, he admittedly meant that American Protestants were "thereby the more easily prejudiced against our claims to their notice." By the word Catholic, Ravenscroft meant it "as used in the Creeds, and applied to the

PART III: INTELLECTUALS

Church of Christ, is to be understood Universal, and Universal is such a sense, as is opposed to national or particular." And the word apostolic he understood to be "the derivation of that authority, which was committed to the Apostles by Christ himself, for the founding, extending, establishing and ordering his Church to the end of the world, and this, in such a sense, as is opposed to every other derivation of authority, whatever." [1]

Ravenscroft knew what biblical, apostolic, and catholic churchly authority looked like. Bishops ruled true churches since the Apostolic era and a true church retained the rule of prelates who traced their ordination back to the apostles. Ravenscroft did not see this as negotiable, and he tied the rule of bishops to orthodoxy. By 1800 the rise of Unitarianism in Calvinist churches provided what Ravenscroft believed was ample proof of the necessity of bishops to guard the true faith and the inevitable doctrinal drift that stemmed from the absence of episcopacy. His own experience with a democratic Wesleyan sect before he became an Episcopalian only strengthened his belief that true churches needed bishops to guard them and defend them from bad theology and ecclesiastical disorder. Ravenscroft's prelacy in North Carolina is typically credited with introducing the High Church tradition into Southern states. Ravenscroft ordained a series of High Church presbyters who went on to exercise ecclesiastically important posts in the Episcopal Church in the South, but Ravenscroft's dispositions were not reflexive appeals to authoritarianism or sectarianism. He identified very real weaknesses in evangelical and Calvinist churches in the early American republic and had good reason to believe that the rule of bishops guarded the Episcopal Church from the theological heresies of the day in the United States; while Unitarianism and Arianism invaded Calvinistic and Wesleyan churches, the Episcopal Church in the era remained firmly on the side of biblical orthodoxy. He also understood broad democratizing trends and their effects on religion in the Early National United States.

---

[1] John Stark Ravenscroft, *To the members of the Protestant Episcopal Church, in St. James's, Mecklenburg County* (Richmond, VA: John Warrock, 1824), 7.

His High Churchmanship stemmed from a commitment to Episcopal church order. So too did his dislike of Calvinism. In both cases Ravenscroft warned about threats to order writ large. In democratized religion—perceived by Ravenscroft to be led in North Carolina and Virginia by Calvinists—he saw ecclesiastical and moral disorder, and he sought to staunch democracy's ostensibly baneful influence throughout his episcopacy.

In some senses, Ravenscroft wasn't even a uniform High Churchman. Richard Rankin in his history of the Episcopal church in antebellum North Carolina notes that Ravenscroft "was far from theologically consistent himself and drew from both theological traditions within the American Episcopal Church—High Church and Low Church." Ravenscroft's "understanding of the salvation process [soteriology] was a variation of the typical evangelical scheme: he believed that an adult believer must have an experience of rebirth before becoming a full, communing member." He told a correspondent that "in general terms I consider confirmation equivalent to a profession of religion on conviction and experience." That he served for years as a rector in the decidedly Low Church Diocese of Virginia strengthened his Evangelical bonafides. Ravenscroft's preaching, Rankin argues, remained decidedly Evangelical, and his tendency to attract women in particular to churches to hear his preaching corresponds more with the preaching tendencies of Evangelical bishops than Tractarian-sympathizing ones. Still, Ravenscroft was undeniably a High Churchman. His High Churchmanship however needs to be understood as a continuation of a commitment to ecclesiastical order rather than the adoption of an innovative philosophy of religious history or a rejection of Protestant soteriology. Ravenscroft was an Old High Churchmen consistent with High Churchmen of the eras preceding the Tractarian controversy more than he was a meaningful disciple of the so-called Oxford Movement.[2]

---

[2] Richard Rankin, *Ambivalent Churchmen and Evangelical Churchwomen: The Religion of the Episcopal Elite in North Carolina, 1800-1860* (Columbia, SC: University of South Carolina Press, 1993), 67-68.

PART III: INTELLECTUALS

Unlike most of the other Episcopal bishops in office between 1789 and the beginning of the American Civil War, Ravenscroft spent a significant time of his childhood in the United Kingdom. When his father left colonial Virginia in 1772, he seemed to have done so without planning to return. There are a variety of reasons why he could have left, but likely one is that the Ravenscroft family had fallen on hard financial times during the late colonial era. John N. Norton, Bishop Ravenscroft's Nineteenth Century biographer, noted that the Ravenscroft family had planned to sell a significant amount of their property as they left for Great Britain, probably to be able to afford life in Scotland where they plan to reside. Whatever financial plans they did have were quickly dashed by the American Revolution and the United States' War of Independence between 1775 and 1781. The family's business dealings were "all arranged" to Dr. Ravsncrofts' "satisfaction, but in consequence of the unsettled state of the country during the war, the payments were not promptly met." Being in debt and struggling at times to meet the demands of creditors led to Dr. Ravenscroft being "somewhat embarrassed during the rest of his life, although he left his widow in easy circumstances. He died towards the close of 1780." [3]

A financially embarrassed father undoubtedly affected the young Ravenscroft. An absent father meant not only financial duress but a harder life in general. Young John Ravenscroft sought solace in his mother, in the Scottish landscapes he frequently took long walks through, and in the Scottish schools he attended. In those Presbyterian-led academies he received what he called "the rudiments of my education." In later life, he felt "bound to record that I owe much to the custom there established of making the Scriptures a school book—a custom, I am grieved to say it, not only abandoned in the schools and academies among us, but denounced as improper, if not injurious." He never noticed in his boyhood "any power or influence over my thoughts or actions thence derived from the scriptures." Nonetheless the "mere

[3] John N. Norton, *The Life of Bishop Ravenscroft* (New York: General Protestant Episcopal Sunday School Union), 15-17

memory retained of their life-giving truths, proved of unspeakable advantage when I became awakened to the subject of religion." As a bishop he recalled "that what was thus unconsciously sown in my heart, though smothered and choked by the levity of youth, and abused and perverted by the negligence and sinfulness of my riper years, was, nevertheless a preparation of Heaven's foresight and mercy." His education in Scotland led "grace to quicken me—a mighty help to my amazed and confounded soul, when brought to a just view of my actual condition as a sinner, both by nature and by practice." Although he attended schools, most likely Presbyterian, that placed the premium on biblical recitation and knowledge, Ravenscroft did not identify with the Church of Scotland nor did his family apparently attend church regularly during his boyhood.

By the time Ravenscroft entered his adolescent years his mother enjoyed a more stable financial situation. John Stark however wanted to reclaim some of his family's former patrimony so with his mother's blessing he returned to the United states in 1789. His mother elected to stay in her native Scotland and never again traveled to the American Republic. Ravenscroft came back to the United States in a heady political and social moment. George Washington served as the American Union's first president and Virginia still claimed her rank as first among equal states. Ravenscroft enrolled in the College of William and Mary but did not impress his peers, the faculty, or himself with what he admitted was a lackluster and mediocre collegiate career. What he did gain at William and Mary were friends and societal cachet he used to better his position in Early Republic Virginia society. Ravenscroft married the daughter of Lewis Burwell and through that connection ensconced himself in Virginia's slave-holding aristocracy. In 1792 he returned briefly to Scotland to check on his mother's condition and to settle some family administrative affairs. It seems to have been the last time he saw his mother.

For the next 18 years Ravenscroft and his wife lived the quiet existence of Virginia's middling gentry. While they were never part of the first rank of Virginia's first families they knew enough local notables to be included in neighborhood socialization and in the small parties thrown on Virginia farms for friends and neighbors. John Norton waxed poetic when he wrote that the future bishop "continued to live—a devoted husband, a kind master, and a good neighbor, and universally respected by all who knew him." Even Norton's relatively hagiographic treatment of Ravenscroft's life before he entered the ministry could not hide the reality of real tragedy for Ravenscroft and his wife. They were "never blessed with any children" of their own, a significant emotional and psychological hardship in a society that valued fecundity and dynatic lineages as much as early Nineteenth Century Virginia did. Nonetheless Ravenscroft "acted the part of a father towards five orphans, who were placed under his care while infants, and no parent could have discharged his duties more conscientiously and faithfully."

In 1810 Ravenscroft experienced some sort of religious conversion. He recounted to friends that he used to ride to the distant portions of his properties regularly. He had become a man of some means and had a sizable plantation. His daily rides were where he thought about higher things, he wrote in a short autobiographical essay, and it was on those rides that he finally became aware of the reality that he was a sinner and his need for a savior. Ravenscroft had never been an active churchgoer so his conversion was neither particularly intellectual, nor was it churchly. He did not read theologically or philosophically. In order to make a public profession of faith he sought out the nearest group of Christians he could find. Eight miles from his plantation there was a meeting house of the Republican Methodists, an egalitarian Wesleyan sect that did not have regular clergymen or particularly ordered worship services. He and his wife worshiped with the Republican Methodists for a few years and it was during that time, between 1810 and 1816, that Ravenscroft began to discern a call to holy orders.

Unlike other churchmen in Virginia, Ravenscroft imbibed a violent dislike of what he perceived as Early Republic Calvinism. He used sermons and letters to deny that the Church of England had any association with what he called the ideas of Calvin proper, as opposed to the broad reception of reformed ideas from the 16th century. Where

Ravenscroft learned his dislike of Calvinist theology is hard to discern from the written record, but it is likely that much of it came from his time in Scotland and from the time spent in an egalitarian Wesleyan community in the years immediately after his conversion to Christianity. But more than anything, Ravenscroft perceived in Calvinist churches and in Presbyterianism in particular a complete lack of order. During his search for a church to join and seek ordination after leaving the Republican Methodists he found all the local sects, "according to my view, acting upon usurped authority." Ravenscroft admitted that he "paused a while on the Presbyterian claim to apostolic succession, but as that claim could date no farther back than the era of the Reformation, and in its first lines labours under the dispute whether it has actually the authority which mere Presbyters can bestow." He complained specifically that "it does not appear satisfactorily that Calvin ever had orders of any kind." Consequently he turned his "attention to the Protestant Episcopal Church for that deposit of apostolic succession, in which alone verifiable power to minister in sacred things was to be found in the United States." Ravenscroft became not merely an Episcopalian, but a virulent High Churchman who believed that episcopacy was necessary to the true church and that the Church of England was the true Catholic church that had been reformed against papal error and innovation in the Sixteenth Century Reformation. Unlike George Washington Doane, John Henry Hobart, and other High Churchmen of the Early Republic, Ravenscroft died before he could engage other Protestants in controversies surrounding the Tractarian movement, but he jousted with other Protestants on questions of baptismal regeneration and ecclesiology.[4]

In a work responding to what he believed were misrepresentations of the Episcopal Church by noted Presbyterian minister and editor

---

[4] Walker Anderson, "Memoir" in *The Works of the Right Reverend John Stark Ravenscroft, D,D.' Bishop of the Protestant Episcopal Church in the Diocese of North Carolina. Containing his Sermons, Charges, and Controversial Tracts; To which is prefixed, a Memoir of his Life* Volume I (New York: Protestant Episcopal Press, 1830), 20

John Holt Rice, Ravenscroft wrote that the Episcopal Church plainly taught that baptism bestowed regeneration, but he added that the word regeneration had been foisted on the Episcopal Church by Calvinists. The church, he argued, "knows nothing of the use of this word in the novel, improper, and unscriptural meaning which Calvinist clings to. Nor is there a stronger proof of the anti-Calvinistic structure of her articles than the baptismal office, as it stands in the liturgy." Ravenscroft quoted Article XXXI and proposed that the Episcopal Church asserted, "with the plain language, primitive interpretation, and general tenor of Scripture, 'that JESUS CHRIST, by the grace of God, tasted death for every man.'" It was not the will of God "that one of these little ones should perish;' so in this initiating sacrament of grace, she asserts of infants absolutely, and adults conditionally, that they are regenerate." Calvinism, he believed, placed the grace of God in direct opposition, so that baptism in the Calvinist system was meaningless. "I make bold to say," he told a potential communicant, "that the wit of man cannot invent a scriptural and reasonable objection to this view of the subject, which is not derived from the Calvinistic views of the nature and effect of divine grace." Calvinist views on nature and grace were "the root from which has sprung the whole difficulty, and out of which has grown the change in the meaning and use of the word regeneration, with all the confusion of mind consequent on the adoption of strange doctrine." Rice's Calvinist doctrine was "as much at war with the word of GOD, and the attributes of Jehovah, as it is abhorrent to the common sense and rewardable condition of moral beings."[5]

The extent to which Ravenscroft actually disliked the actual theological legacy of John Calvin is confusing. After excoriating Rice and Virginia's Presbyterians for their version of Calvinism, he argued that John Calvin actually believed that baptism was regenerative. What

---

[5] John Stark Ravenscroft, "The Doctrines of the Church Vindicated from the Misrepresentations of Dr John Rice; And the Integrity of Revealed Religion Defended against the 'No Comment Principle' of Promiscuous Bible Societies" in *The Works of the Right Reverend John Stark Ravenscroft* Volume I, 353-54.

he seemed to object to was doctrines of eternal security that annihilated the baptized person's ability to "work out their faith with fear and trembling." Like many Early Republic Episcopalians, Ravenscroft feared rising antinomianism. To his views on ecclesiology and the need for order he coupled with a rejection of doctrines of eternal security as it was posited by North American Calvinists in the first half of the Nineteenth Century. Against Rice, Ravenscroft quoted John Calvin's *Institutes* and suggested that Calvin supported baptismal regeneration. That doctrine, argued Ravenscroft, was "in the very teeth of the express declarations of your far-famed and honoured founder, of your own fundamentals, and of every reputable platform of Christian faith." However strange baptismal regeneration might be to Rice and his fellow Presbyterians, Calvin, Reformed confessions, and all true churches all asserted "in the plainest terms, the inseparable union of the grace of regeneration with the Christian sacrament of baptism."[6]

North Carolina's Bishop had another reason to dislike Early Republic Southern Presbyterians. Beginning in the 1780s and continuing into the Early Republic, Presbyterians and Baptists in Virginia had looked to the Commonwealth government to reduce the prestige of the Episcopal Church. John Norton, a well-known biographer of Episcopal bishops in the Nineteenth Century, conceded that there was "an honest prejudice against the Episcopal Church in the minds of many, in consequence of its being the form of religion which had been established by the English government." Dissenters—Baptists, Methodists, and Presbyterians—"fancied, in their ignorance, that this Church could have no existence except as connected with the mother country." The fact that "Washington, the leader of the American armies, and not a few of the noblest sons of Virginia, whose patriotism could not be questioned, never relaxed their attachment for the Episcopal Church, in whose bosom they lived and died" should have opened the eyes of the dissenters and "convinced them" of their errors. But such, unfortunately, was not the case. Baptists and Methodists, and other denominations, "had

[6] *Ibid.*

always been hostile to the Episcopal Church, because it was the established religion of the kingdom." After 1776 when "the colonies were free, and all forms of religion stood on the same platform in the eye of the law," Evangelical dissenters "put forth every effort to destroy it, root and branch." Through "artful management they contrived to have several laws adopted by the legislature of Virginia, which should have a tendency to further their views." Those views unambiguously committed dissenters to attacking Anglicanism's legacy, ecclesiastical, legal, and social. Church property in particular was an easy target.[7]

Particularly galling to Episcopalians at the time of disestablishment and later was the naked land grab perpetrated by dissenters and Thomas Jefferson's Republicans in the Virginia assembly who passed a law that "formally declared, that 'the title to the property the Church had held before the Revolution was vested in the State at large; and that, whenever they were vacant, the glebes should be sold for the benefit of the poor of the parish.'" It was under the guise of disestablishment that "those acts which always mark confiscation followed. The glebes were sold at prices merely nominal, and the small sums which did accrue from them flowed into various channels of private profit." Anglican "churchyards, and the churches with their furniture, were exempted from the operations of this law; yet they, and even the communion-plate, were seized and sold." Although Evangelical dissenters undoubtedly viewed this as completely compatible with the legacy of the American Revolution, many Anglicans, Ravenscroft included, believed that the Evangelicals were doing nothing more than adopting the power of this state to weaponize so-called disestablishment against Anglicanism. John Holt Rice implied in his magazine that Anglican claims that the true church was an Episcopal Church were un-American and would eventually harm republican society in the United States. Episcopacy, Rice argued, was "at war with the best interests of religion, and with the true genius of our institutions; and we regard it as a solemn duty to oppose them in

---

[7] John N. Norton, *The Life of the Right Reverend Richard Channing Moore, D. D., Bishop of Virginia* (New York: General Protestant Episcopal S. School Union and Church Book Society, 1857), 38-39.

every way consistent with the character of Christians." For Rice and his Presbyterians, there was no room left for *de jure divino* Episcopalians in the new disestablished American order.[8]

Rice's Presbyterians and other Evangelicals, through print media like *The Christian Monitor* and *The Virginia Evangelical and Literary Magazine* that Rice Rice edited, associated Evangelical religion with republican government. Presbyterians and even more egalitarian Baptists and Methodists refrained from unqualified defenses of political democracy, but they nonetheless embraced the broad tenor of societal and religious democratization. Episcopal bishops and rectors worried constantly about the forces of democracy and democracy's effect on society and religion. What one Episcopal rector called the alliance of Evangelicalism and egalitarianism convinced churchmen like Ravenscroft that a more forceful defense of the church and its apostolic (and undemocratic) constitution was needed. "That the church is divine in its origin, and in the appointments connected with it, is so generally admitted a doctrine, that the less may suffice on this point; yet it ought ever to be borne in mind, that this divine institution of the wisdom and goodness of God, is not an abstract idea to be entertained in the mind." The Episcopal church was "an actual, visible, accessible body or society, for practical use; deriving its constitution, laws and authority, directly from God." God placed the church, governed by prelates who inherited their authority from the apostles, "beyond the reach of any human appointment, addition, or alteration; and this so strictly, that all the wisdom, piety, and authority in the world, congregated together, is just as incompetent to originate a Church, as to call another universe into existence." No matter how popular new religious associations might be, Ravenscroft made clear they were not true churches. More likely, he feared, they were forces of religious disorder.[9]

[8] *Ibid.*
[9] John Holt Rice, "A Discourse Delivered before the Literary and Philosophical Society of Hampden-Sydney College, at their Anniversary Meeting, on the 24th of September 1824" in *The Virginia Literary and Evangelical Magazine* 8 (1825): 1-18; Nathan O. Hatch, *The Democratization of American Christianity* (New Haven, CT: Yale University Press, 1989), 21;John Stark

PART III: INTELLECTUALS

Order, and the strength to impose order, motivated Ravenscroft to take a firm hand with immorality and with disordered morality and religion in his diocese. Ravenscroft was a big man, over six feet tall and weighing over 220 pounds. He practiced his theology "in the face of unfriendly neighbors." The Diocese of North Carolina needed what Episcopal historian Frank McLean called "muscular Christianity" in order to control "the godless element that swarmed the rivers and cheated, fought, and died in the raw country from which they sought to grasp temporal fortunes." Democratized Carolinians treated Ravenscoft with contempt, "bred naturally from ignorance," even as the bishop "worked patiently among them, not for an earthly but for a heavenly treasure." Ravenscroft's firmness took physical forms at times. His protege Bishop Green of Mississippi related an encounter that the Bishop had in a stagecoach where he threatened to physically throw an obviously inebriated man out if he did not cease using profanity around the other passengers. "Utter another oath, sir, if you dare," bellowed the bishop, "and I will throw you under the wheels of the coach!"[10]

Duties as a bishop and the experience of being a widower twice took an emotional and physical toll on Ravenscroft. His second wife died in 1829, and the bishop, never in good health, threw himself into a succession of episcopal visits that took him as far afield as Kentucky and Tennessee. The visits and other ministerial labours would be his undoing. Bishop Ravenscroft died in March, 1830. During his prelacy he placed his mark on the Episcopal Church in newer Southern states through his mentorship of James Hervey Otey and William Mercer Green, later bishops of Tennessee and Mississippi, respectively. Ravenscroft inherited a tiny diocese, weak in numbers of communicants and in parishes. He grew it into a respectable diocese that sent priests—like Bishop Otey and Bishop Green—south and west to other regions of

Ravenscroft, "A Sermon on the Church; Delivered Before the Annual Convention of the Protestant Episcopal Church of North-Carolina," in *The Works of the Right Reverend John Stark Ravenscroft*, 97.

[10] Frank M. McClain, "The Theology of Bishops Ravenscroft, Otey, and Green Concerning the Church, the Ministry, and the Sacraments." *Historical Magazine of the Protestant Episcopal Church* 33, no. 2 (1964): 103–36.

the United States. Ravenscroft, unlike the Virginia bishops he served under before he became a bishop, never tempered ecclesiastical claims in the service of making the Episcopal Church more palatable for the United States' republican and increasingly democratic social and religious society. The regenerative nature of baptism and the necessity of episcopal ordination for apostolic succession remained foundational for what Ravenscroft perceived as marks of the true church. It is a testament to his legacy that the Deep South's Episcopal dioceses mirrored his High Church image more than that of the Low Church bishops of Virginia. Ravenscroft, more than any other Southern bishop, helped create the High Churchmanship that still typifies large swaths of Anglican churches in the South in the Twenty-First Century.[11]

---

[11] *Sketches of Church History in North Carolina: Addresses and Papers by Clergymen and Laymen of the Dioceses of North and East Carolina* (Wilmington, NC: William L. De Rosset, 1892), 211-212; William Stevens Perry, *The Episcopate in America: Sketches, Biographical and Bibliographical, of the Bishops of the American Church, with a Preliminary Essay on the Historic Episcopate and Documentary Annals of the Anglican Line of Succession into America* (New York: The Christian Literature Co., 1895), 47.

Charles McIlvaine
1799-1873

"Bishop McIlvaine is a man of a thousand; he unites a force and unction rarely found together."[1] So wrote Charles Sumner, a Church of England bishop, encouraging a friend to meet the man and his family who then were visiting England in 1853.

Charles Pettit McIlvaine was indeed a man of particular power and piety. He served as bishop of Ohio for over forty years, from his consecration in the Fall of 1832 to his death in the Spring of 1873. The man did much more than shepherd a growing and important diocese within the Protestant Episcopal Church. He led a life of theological struggle. In these contests, he became the leading American articulator and defender of the Evangelical party within the Protestant Episcopal Church.

His prominence did not end on the shores of his own country but spread to Great Britain, a place he traveled to often and whose own Evangelicals republished his works to much acclaim. In the Preface to an English publication of one of his later works, Bishop Samuel Waldengrave wrote that McIlvaine "has already been for many years known amongst us as one who has, by his writings and his example, done good service in the illustration and vindication of Scriptural and Apostolic doctrine and practice. Any new work from his pen must, therefore, from

---

[1] Quoted in Charles Pettit McIlvaine, *Memorials of the Right Reverend Charles Pettit McIlvaine*, edited by William Carus (New York: Thomas Whittaker, 1882), 143.

the well-earned reputation of his former books, command the hopeful attention of English Christians."[2]

McIlvaine was born on January 18, 1799, in Burlington, New Jersey. He came from a prominent family that included a military secretary to George Washington and a governor of New Jersey. His father, Joseph, was a well-respected lawyer and served as a United States Senator from 1823 until his death in August of 1826.[3] Charles's parents took him to worship at St. Mary's parish, the Episcopal Church in Burlington. The parish's rector, Charles Henry Wharton, was a prominent clergyman, a Roman Catholic priest who had converted to Protestantism and who had become known both for his poetry and his polemical works debating Roman clergy. Though they attended services, both father and mother seemed irreligious in McIlvaine's childhood. Neither parent was baptized, much less confirmed in the Church until much later in Charles' life; and, consequently, neither mother nor father presented infant Charles for baptism.[4]

As had two brothers before him and as would two after, McIlvaine enrolled at the College of New Jersey (now Princeton) at the age of 15. He intended to enter the law profession as his father had done.[5] However, a work of God altered those plans. McIlvaine traced his conversion to Christianity to an 1815 revival at Princeton, the year after his matriculation.[6] He later recounted that "[i]n that precious season of the power of God, my religious life began" and that "I had *heard* before; I began then to know."[7] No doubt with later disputes over revival in mind,

---

[2] Samuel Waldegrave, "Preface to the English Edition," in Charles Pettit McIlvaine, *The True Temple* (Philadelphia: Protestant Episcopal Book Society, 1861), v.

[3] Richard W. Smith, *Bishop McIlvaine, Slavery, Britain, & the Civil War* (Bloomington, IN: Xlibris, 2014), 1-2.

[4] Diana Hochstedt Butler, *Standing Against the Whirlwind: Evangelical Episcopalians in Nineteenth Century America* (Oxford University Press, 1995), 24.

[5] Loren Dale Pugh, *Bishop Charles Pettit McIlvaine: The Faithful Evangel*, PhD Diss., (New York: Duke University, 1985), 10.

[6] Thomas GarrettIsham, *A Born Again Episcopalian: The Evangelical Witness of Charles P. McIlvaine* (Port St. Lucie, FL: Solid Ground Christian Books, 2011), 20-21.

[7] McIlvaine, *Memorials*, 11.

McIlvaine described this awakening at Princeton as, "quiet, unexcited, and entirely free from all devices or means, beyond the few and simple which God has appointed, namely, prayer and the ministry of the Word."[8] Through these means, God forever brought McIlvaine into His Church. Reverend Wharton then baptized McIlvaine back at St. Mary's in Burlington.[9]

At Princeton, the young man made friends with Charles Hodge, the future giant of American Presbyterianism, as well as John Johns, a future Episcopal bishop for the Diocese of Virginia.[10] In collaboration with these and other men, McIlvaine started some of America's earliest Sunday Schools, four in the Princeton area and another in his hometown of Burlington. The Burlington school in particular thrived, tripling in size in a short time and showing early on McIlvaine's skills as a teacher.[11]

McIlvaine graduated from College of New Jersey at the top of his class in December of 1816. He had determined then to pursue the diaconate and the priesthood within the Protestant Episcopal Church. With those plans in view, the following year he entered the seminary at Princeton, which was not an Episcopal school, grounded instead in the Presbyterian tradition. Thus, to supplement studies assigned in class, McIlvaine received, with institutional approval, additional works focused on his own theological tradition assigned by William White, one of the original bishops of the Protestant Episcopal Church following the American Revolution.[12] However, ill health cut short his institutional theological training, requiring him to return to Burlington to recuperate. Back home, he completed his studies with Charles Warren in preparation for entering Holy Orders. McIlvaine subsequently received ordination to the diaconate in 1820, then the priesthood in 1823.

[8] *Ibid.*
[9] *Ibid.*, 9.
[10] Butler, 24
[11] Isham, 17-18.
[12] *Ibid.*, 67. These White-assigned works were light on Reformation era writers and heavy on the Carolingian divines.

He immediately joined the ecclesiastical divisions of the time. The Protestant Episcopal Church then consisted mostly of two parties known as "High Church" and "Low Church" or "Evangelical." In the 1820s and 1830s, their differences concerned issues such as whether bishops were necessary for valid ordination and thus for the dispensing of valid sacraments. Along similar lines, the two camps diverged on the usefulness and rightness of working across denominational lines, with the "High" party against doing so and the "Evangelical" generally in favor. This point played into whether some meetings could occur which did not only use assigned liturgy from the Prayer Book, with Evangelicals being generally open and High Churchmen opposed.

One useful example of this division in McIlvaine's early ministry came in 1827. McIlvaine received an invitation to preach at a St. Paul's parish in Rochester, New York. Rev. Henry U. Onderdonk, High Churchman and future bishop of Pennsylvania, wrote a letter to the parish's vestry advising them against allowing McIlvaine to give a sermon. It accused McIlvaine of being so low as to be a "half-churchman, a great opponent of Bishop Hobart [New York leader of High Church party], and a zealous promoter of schemes that would blend us with Presbyterians."[13] This letter then was published in a Philadelphia newspaper.[14] McIlvaine wrote and had published an extended response to these accusations. In it, we see early on his understanding of what defined the Protestant Episcopal Church. McIlvaine declared himself committed to the rightness of Episcopacy, though he argued against *"the exclusive divine right of* Episcopacy"[15] that would declare illegitimate other Protestant ministers' ordination or their administration of the sacraments invalid. He affirmed his high view of and fidelity to the Church's liturgy, calling it the, "best ever composed, or likely to be composed by man."[16] He continued that he would oppose the introduction

---

[13] Reprinted in "Rev. Mr. McIlvaine in Answer to the Rev. H.U. Onderdonk" (Philadelphia: William Stavley, 1827), 4.
[14] Butler, 45-46.
[15] McIlvaine, "Rev. Mr. McIlvaine in Answer," 13.
[16] *Ibid.*

of any other liturgy and, when officiating, "in circumstances such as, in his opinion, were contemplated in the prescription of the liturgy, it is his settled principle to use every item of the regular service, without omitting or adding one word."[17] Still, in Evangelical fashion, he argued there were times when Christians could gather together for prayer meetings and like functions even if no particular liturgy existed for them. Moreover, McIlvaine declared the truth of and his obedience to the other Formularies of the Church, including the Articles of Religion as well as the Homilies. Their status as formularies would prove deeply important for his ministry throughout. Finally, he defended his ecumenical relations with other Protestants, declaring them in line with the practice of the historic Church of England as well as the short history of the Protestant Episcopal Church.

McIlvaine's talents were recognized early. Even before becoming a deacon, McIlvaine received his first call. It came from Christ Church in Georgetown. There, his powerful preaching attracted the attention of notable men in the National government such as the Secretary of War, John C. Calhoun, and Kentucky Senator Henry Clay.[18]

While in the D.C. area, McIlvaine aided in the composition of the *Washington Theological Repertory*. This journal was founded in 1819 by William Wilmer, rector of St. Paul's Church in Alexandria, VA. Other participants included Rev. William Meade, later bishop of Virginia. The publication sought to articulate the Evangelical perspective of the Protestant Episcopal Church, views in line with McIlvaine's later defense against Onderdonk. Its claims also elicited controversy. In 1822, McIlvaine helped compose a defense of the Episcopal clergy in D.C. against criticisms based largely on the *Repertory* and like writings. Bishop James Kemp had accused the clergy in the D.C. area of, among other things, being Calvinists.[19] While the response denied they held

---

[17] *Ibid.*
[18] Kara M. McClurken, "For Love of God and Country," in *Anglican and Episcopal History* 69(3)(September 2000) 322.
[19] "Letter to the Right Rev. James Kemp in Defense of the Clergy of the District of Columbia" (Washington: WM Duncan, 1822).

to the "doctrines of *particular redemption and unconditional reprobation*," McIlvaine aligned himself and his fellow clergy with the Reformational giants of the Church of England, including "Witgift...Jewell...Ridley...Hall...Usher." Those divines did hold to a reformed theology, and the document confidently declared that if those churchmen were Calvinists, "then are we Calvinists."[20]

During this time in D.C., McIlvaine twice served as chaplain to the United States Congress, for the second session of the 17th and the same for the 18th.[21] That time overlapped with his father's tenure in the Senate, which must have been a point of pride for both father and son. However, McIlvaine did not remain long in his D.C. call. In January of 1825, McIvaine accepted a position as chaplain and teacher of ethics at West Point, where he served from 1825 to the end of 1827.

McIlvaine found West Point a spiritual desert. By his own recounting, the only professed believers at the institution when he arrived were three wives of other instructors.[22] After a year in which no cadet or professor showed interest in Christianity, McIlvaine finally saw fruit borne. One cadet came to him professing a sudden work of the Spirit in his heart. Others followed, until McIlvaine perceived a remarkable work of God that brought many cadets and several faculty into the church. The revival at West Point both enlarged his reputation among Evangelicals in the Church and excited opposition among the High Churchmen.

Beyond the awakening at West Point, McIlvaine grew in fame through a work of apologetics, *The Evidences of Christianity*.[23] The book was based on a series of lectures he gave in New York City in the Winter of 1831-1832. It met with great success, both in the States and in England, going through many editions and including several updates from McIlvaine.

---

[20] "In Defense of the Clergy," 22.
[21] McIlvaine, *Memorials*, 17.
[22] Butler, 39.
[23] Charles P. McIlvaine, *The Evidences of Christianity* (New York: Collins and Hannay, 1833).

With this newfound notoriety, McIlvaine entertained a number of requests to serve as rector, one which included with it the presidency of William & Mary College. He eventually accepted a call to St. Ann's in Brooklyn. During this time, he struggled with other parts of the diocese, including his bishop, John Henry Hobart. These struggles again concerned the debates between High Church and Evangelical distinctives within the Protestant Episcopal Church.

But McIlvaine did not long remain within the New York diocese. In 1831, the Diocese of Ohio elected him their second bishop in response to the resignation of Philander Chase. Some controversy ensued as to whether the bishop's seat had truly been vacated with the division falling largely along party lines. However, McIlvaine's call eventually was approved. Bishops William White, William Meade, and John Henry Hobart consecrated McIlvaine Bishop of the Diocese of Ohio on October 31, 1832.[24]

He took over a diocese that had grown significantly under Bishop Chase. But it still remained relatively scant in resources, clergy, and parishioners. That would change over the next forty years under the care of the new bishop. As he and his diocese continued to grow in stature, McIlvaine became the clear leader of the Evangelical set within the Protestant Episcopal Church. In this role, he acquired friends with the same party within the Church of England, making frequent trips there. He especially admired the ministry of Charles Simeon, whom he had the chance to meet and converse with on several occasions.[25] In fact, so well known was McIvlaine's affection for the English priest that, upon Simeon's death, McIvaine was gifted his cassock.[26]

In his leadership position, McIlvaine took a commanding role in the theological and ecclesiastical battles then occurring within the Protestant Episcopal Church and in the Church of England. In the

---

[24] Butler, 61-63.
[25] See especially McIlvaine, "Introduction to the American Edition" in *Memoirs of the Life of the Rev. Charles Simeon,* edited by William Carus (New York: Robert Carter, 1847).
[26] Butler, 31.

1830s, he sought to defend the possibility of revival along the lines of which he had witnessed at West Point. At the same time, he saw in Ohio the ills and excesses that could attend revivals. He guarded against these tendencies in his diocese as the Second Great Awakening grew, at times even being willing to work with High Churchmen in response. In an early charge to the clergy of his diocese, he said such revivals must be led by ordained persons and that they must maintain adherence to the liturgy of the Prayer Book. He gave similar instructions to lay persons. Early in his bishopric, he wrote a letter to an Ohio parish experiencing revival. He gave numerous criteria for how such a work of God should look. He advised them to be watchful and to be "sober-minded." He added, "[l]et all noise and all endeavours to promote mere animal feeling be shunned."[27] He said, in similar fashion to what he wrote to the clergy, "[i]f any think they have advanced so far in religion that they cannot relish the Liturgy, they have been learning elsewhere than at the feet of Jesus, and have received some spirit besides that which is of God."[28]

However, McIlvaine spent much of his bishopric engaging with the Oxford Movement from England. McIlvaine saw this movement gaining influence in the Protestant Episcopal Church starting in the late 1830s. He proved a focused and ferocious critic, writing extensively against its doctrines, practices, and persons. In fact, most of his writings from 1840 onwards bore some connection to engaging John Henry Newman, Edward Pusey, and their adherents stateside. He began with, and made central to his response, the doctrine of justification by faith alone, which he asserted the Oxford Movement rejected in a move toward Roman Catholicism. His first salvo came in a charge delivered to the clergy of his diocese in 1839, the text of which he published the following year.[29] There, he argued that man's justification before God was imputed only, not infused. While not mentioning the Tractarians directly, he later noted that he penned the charge with their views in mind.

[27] McIlvaine, *Memorials*, 82.
[28] *Ibid.*, 83.
[29] McIlvaine, *Justification by Faith* (Columbus, OH: Isaac N. Whiting, 1840).

Direct engagement came soon afterward. In 1841, he published an entire book, *Oxford Divinity Compared with that of the Romish and Anglican Churches.*[30] Focusing again on the doctrine of justification, it became the standard work refuting the Tractarians on both sides of the Atlantic. Daniel Wilson, the Bishop to Calcutta, called *Oxford Divinity* "the best book that had appeared since the Reformation."[31] While hyperbolic, that compliment showed the influence of the book. It proved a powerful work bolstering the Evangelical (and even co-belligerent High Churchmen) in this ongoing debate.

McIlvaine, though, did not stop his critique with the issue of Justification. He saw broader threats to the Episcopal Church in this movement which subsequent works developed. In 1846, he published why he would not consecrate a parish in his diocese that had an altar rather than a table, believing it now wrongly gave impressions of transubstantiation in the administration of Holy Communion.[32] In 1861, he published a work on the nature of the Church called *The True Temple.*[33] He grounded this discussion in the distinction between the visible and invisible Church. The visible Church consisted of those who publicly professed faith in Christ, received baptism, and partook of Holy Communion. The invisible church consisted of those who truly were regenerated—united to Christ by faith, justified in Him also through faith, and now being sanctified by the inward work of the Holy Spirit. McIlvaine believed that both elements of the High Church faction and the Oxford Movement had sought to conflate the two too much. This conflation mattered greatly because, "[t]hey affect the whole system of Gospel doctrine" materially changing the "answer to the question, *What is it to be a*

---

[30] McIlvaine, *Oxford Divinity* (Philadelphia: Joseph Whetham & Son, 1841).
[31] Recounted in a letter to McIlvaine by his son, Joseph. See *Memorials*, 126. He received extensive praise on both sides of the Atlantic for this work as well. See Butler, 107-108.
[32] See Charles Pettit McIlvaine, *Reasons for Refusing to Consecrate a Church Having an Alter Instead of a Communion Table* (New York: Standford & Swords, 1846).
[33] Charles Pettis McIlvaine, *The True Temple; or The Holy Catholic Church and Communion of Saints, in Its Nature, Structure, and Unity* (Philadelphia: Protestant Episcopal Book Society, 1861).

Christian."³⁴ These other camps argued, McIlvaine said, that baptism, in some sense, necessarily conferred the grace of regeneration. They argued that all who consumed the bread and wine at the Lord's Supper truly received Christ. McIlvaine responded that the conflation of the visible and invisible church, with these attendant doctrines regarding the sacraments, involved "the confounding of the form of godliness with its power, and the substitution of a religion of external signs and ordinances for that inward and spiritual grace in the heart without which we are dead before God."³⁵

In the 1860s, McIlvaine added one last target for his writings: the "Broad Churchmen." This movement, also starting in England, sought to downplay doctrine in holding the Church together. It also partook of a kind of rationalism, with some questioning the authority of Scripture as well as the veracity of miracles. It formed an early manifestation of elements against which the later Fundamentalist Movement would react. In 1865, the House of Bishops published a pastoral letter composed by McIlvaine on this matter. It targeted in particular a collected volume written by seven English churchmen entitled, *Essays and Reviews*.³⁶ McIlvaine celebrated that these infidelities for so long had not penetrated the Episcopal Church. He attributed this success to being "fenced about…by ancient creeds, and by 'articles of religion,' as well as by the required use of a common liturgy, wherein the profession and inculcation of distinctive Gospel truth is wrought into the whole texture of our daily public worship."³⁷ Yet *Essays and Reviews*, widely in circulation in the States, posited a number of claims undermining the Church's doctrine and the underlying authority of Scripture. As he had done against the Tractarians, McIlvaine responded with the essential nature of the core Protestant doctrines that had defined the English Reformation and, he argued, continued to define both the Church of England and the Protestant Episcopal Church.

---

34   McIlvaine, *True Temple*, v. Emphasis in original.
35   *Ibid.*, vi.
36   *Essays and Reviews* (London: John W. Parker and Sons, 1860).
37   McIlvaine, *Rationalism*, 4.

Finally, McIlvaine's tenure as bishop also included the American Civil War from 1861-1865. McIlvaine sided strongly with the Union cause. In the Fall of 1862, the College of Bishops, which then lacked most of the Southern delegation, issued a pastoral letter written by McIlvaine regarding the conflict. McIlvaine exposited Romans 13 as a general and forceful demand to obey the magistrates whom God had placed in power. The letter thus concluded that, "[t]he refusal of such allegiance we hold to be a sin; and when it stands forth in armed rebellion, it is a great crime before the laws of God, as well as man."[38]

McIlvaine also took on a diplomatic role in his support of the Union efforts. Setting sail on November 23, 1861, and staying into 1862, McIlvaine served as an unofficial agent for the national government in England. Leading up to the visit, Great Britain seemed inching closer to recognizing the Confederacy's claims to independence. McIlvaine's mission, one given by no less than Secretary of State William Seward, Treasury Secretary Salmon Chase, and President Abraham Lincoln, was to speak against Great Britain's recognition of the Confederacy with Church of England clergy and others in high positions.[39] McIlvaine had developed friendships not only with many English churchmen but also others in elite circles, including the Prince of Wales, the future Edward VII. When McIlvaine arrived in London, the city and the country were ablaze about the so-called *Trent Affair*, where a United States vessel had intercepted a British ship and removed two Confederate diplomats from it as contraband of war. This alleged violation of Britain's rights threatened to bring about not only English recognition of the Confederacy but potential belligerency between the United States' and British governments. McIlvaine thus worked on the narrower front of addressing English anger over the *Trent* issue and the broader one of advocating for Great Britain to not politically recognize the South. McIlvaine conducted his diplomatic mission with a patriotic intensity, preaching frequently and meeting with important figures in British society to

---

[38] McIlvaine, "Pastoral Letter of the Bishops of the Protestant Episcopal Church" (New York: Baker & Goodwin, 1862), 9.
[39] McClurken, 328.

make the case for the Union. While far from the only factor, McIlvaine's efforts contributed mightily to keeping England on the sidelines for the duration of the conflict.[40] Though tenacious in his defense of the Northern cause, McIlvaine then would show seek to restore the Southern part of the church back into the fold once the war ended.

The closing years of McIlvaine's life saw continued strife within the Protestant Episcopal Church. The battles over doctrine and liturgy brewing for decades would result in the formation of the Reformed Episcopal Church, which in 1873 broke away from the main body in an attempt to remove the developments of the Tractarians and other recent movements. McIlvaine opposed the stirrings of these moves, arguing for Evangelical Episcopalians to remain and to fight. He would not live to see that split occur, however. McIlvaine passed away while visiting Florence, Italy, on March 13, 1873.

McIlvaine left behind a massive legacy. During his bishopric, the Diocese of Ohio showed impressive growth. In McIlvaine's over 40 years as bishop, Ohio's population nearly tripled, from 900,000 to just under 2.7 million. During that time, the diocese nearly tripled in number of parishes (40 to 116), grew from 900 confirmed parishioners to 15,000, and from 17 ordained clergy to 108.[41]

McIlvaine's leadership of the Evangelical wing of the Church, both in the States and in England, also showed his impressive gifts. Throughout his writings defending this view, Bishop McIlvaine articulated a churchmanship grounded in the Protestant Reformation and committed to the Formularies which summarized and preserved them. He quoted generously from the Thirty-Nine Articles as well as the Books of Homilies. On the opening page of the first *Washington Theological Repertory*, the editors stated that "[t]he principles upon which" the publication would work "are those of the Bible, as illustrated in the Articles, Liturgy, and Homilies of the Protestant Episcopal Church."[42] Those commitments summed up McIlvaine's own. He also showed

[40] Isham, 212-213.
[41] Ibid., 8.
[42] *Washington Theological Repertory*, I: 1.

extensive knowledge of earlier divines within the Church of England, quoting extensively from the works of Richard Hooker, Jeremy Taylor, William Perkins, Joseph Hall, and James Ussher. They were his spiritual fathers and he claimed to adhere in his ministry to their doctrinal and liturgical views.

In addition to these controversies, Bishop McIvlaine also was a powerful preacher. In a eulogy, Bishop Alfred Lee of Delaware declared of McIlvaine, "None would question his right to be ranked among the foremost preachers of the day."[43] In addition to preaching himself, McIlvaine emphasized its power and importance. He titled his first charge to the Ohio clergy, "On the Preaching of Christ Crucified." In a consecration sermon for another bishop, McIvlaine declared that "The great duty of the Christian ministry is to *preach*."[44] He followed this sermon up with a charge to the clergy in his diocese titled, "The Work of Preaching Christ" which he expanded into a longer pamphlet for aspiring ministers toward the end of his life, in 1871. The preacher, McIlvaine said, must focus on Christ, "as taught in the Scriptures and set before us in the example of the Apostles."[45] He believed fervently that God worked through the reading and expositing of His Word and sought its power to enliven hearts and to protect the Church against error.

McIlvaine once wrote that the hymn, "Just as I Am" "contains my religion, my theology, my hope….When I am gone, I wish to be remembered in association with that hymn."[46] Its total reliance on God's grace and mercy, as promised in Scripture, stated well Bishop McIlvaine's trust in his sovereign Lord:

> "Just as I am, without one plea
> But that Thy blood was shed for me
> And that Thou bid'st me come to Thee
> Oh, Lamb of God, I come, I come."

[43] Quoted in McIlvaine, *Memorials*, 100.
[44] Charles Pettit McIlvaine, "The Christian Minister's Great Work" (Cincinnati: H.W. Derby & Co., 1850), 15
[45] McIlvaine, *The Work of Preaching Christ* (Boston: Gospel Book & Tract Company, 1871), 4.
[46] See also Butler, 26.

John Henry Hopkins
1792-1868

The Episcopal tradition in the Twenty-first Century is a fairly eclectic one to say the least. It includes camps or "streams" that identify as Evangelical, High Church, Anglo-Catholic, Charismatic, and Progressive, among others. Some persons tend to see themselves as exclusively part of one subset. Others place their feet in more than one, seeking a kind of syncretism.

John Henry Hopkins, the first bishop for the Diocese of Vermont, would seem at home with that last group. He had a love for ornate beauty, both visual and auditory, and insisted on its rightful place within the worship of the Protestant Episcopal Church. Along similar lines, he defended the heightening levels of ceremony that took hold in the United States after the Oxford Movement, even predicting that this form of worship would come to dominate. He held a high view of the episcopal form of government and was resistant to ecumenical relations with other traditions. He studied the Church Fathers extensively, quoted them at length, and thought them of high authority when discussing questions of theology, worship, and practice.

On the other hand, he fiercely defended the Reformation heritage of the Protestant Episcopal Church. He believed Scripture the final authority for matters of faith, defending that position as in line also with the Fathers. He criticized the Roman Catholic Church's views on many fronts, including its understanding of the Papacy, the Eucharist, its treatment of Mary and the saints, and its view of tradition. Finally, he sought a broad tent within the Protestant Episcopal Church, defending the right of certain clergy to believe different from himself so long as those differing views were within the Church's formularies. Prior to his death in 1868, he perceived and in many ways welcomed the coming, increasing diversification within the Protestant Episcopal Church and attempts to at the same time maintain both that diversity and a unified polity.

John Henry Hopkins was born in Dublin, Ireland, on January 30th, 1792. He was the only child of Thomas and Elizabeth Hopkins. Thomas's family had emigrated from England a century before; Elizabeth's father served as a tutor at Trinity College.[1] His paternal grandmother raised him from his weaning until he was six years old.[2] When Hopkins returned to live with his parents, he experienced the joys of a brilliant and doting mother. Elizabeth imparted to her only son her love of education and the arts, which at an early age included readings of William Shakespeare and Alexander Pope, exposure to the music of Haydn, and learning to speak and read French. But the boy also experienced the marital discord between Elizabeth and Hopkins' father. In the only full biography of his father, John, Jr. attributed this friction in large part to two related factors. First, he referenced the differences in intellectual ability and educational achievement between the brilliant wife and the more ordinary husband. Second, he alluded to the wife's willingness to focus on and note those differences. Eventually, Hopkins' parents would separate, never to reconcile in this life.

Hopkins received little religious instruction except for his grandmother requiring him to say a short prayer before bed. His parents would occasionally take him to church but pursued nothing else on matters of faith and practice. Only later in life, with God working through John Henry's efforts, would both mother and father become communicating members of the church.

---

[1] John Henry Hopkins, Jr., *The Life of the Late Right Reverend John Henry Hopkins* (New York: F.J. Huntington & Co., 1873), 21-22.

[2] John Henry Hopkins, III, "John Henry Hopkins, First Bishop of Vermont" *Historical Magazine of the Protestant Episcopal Church* 6(2)(June 1937): 188

The Hopkins family immigrated to the United States in August of 1800. They followed his Uncle John, Thomas's older brother, who reported America as a land of opportunity. The family moved to Philadelphia, where Thomas failed to establish a profitable business and Elizabeth successfully created a thriving school. Young John continued his education while he and his mother began attending St. Peter's in Philadelphia. Bishop William White served as rector. Though sitting under a powerful conduit of the Gospel message, no religious inclinations arose for the young man at this time.

At age fifteen, Hopkins tried working at a counting-house for a year. Though a promising line of work, he declined to continue due to intensely disliking the job. Hopkins at this time considered a life in law, a path his mother strongly encouraged. However, he remained largely uninterested in this vocation as well. His move in a third direction, toward ordained ministry, developed over an extended period of time. Perhaps one can trace its first moments to when atheist friends pushed their views hard on the young man. In response, Hopkins spent two years closely analyzing arguments against God's existence and Christianity's veracity, then turned to examining works defending both.[3] Through these efforts, Hopkins became intellectually convinced of Christianity's truth, though looking back he would not consider himself yet a believer.

The study of law did grow in his estimation during this period and he began seriously considering entering that field. However, his friends, while failing on matters of faith, did convince him on this front, persuading him not to study law but to enter into the iron manufacturing business. They assured him of its good prospects for a secure financial state. Largely smitten on those counts, he dove into its study and practice.

Around this period, Hopkins met his future wife. He came across a family walking along a road in Western Pennsylvania after abandoning their wagon to the thick mud. Melusina Muller was the daughter of

[3] Hopkins, Jr., 31-32.

those German immigrants who had fled Napoleon's conquest of Hamburg only to have their lives in the Baltimore area upended by the British invasion during the War of 1812. (Bunkered down, they listened to the bombing of Fort McHenry about which Francis Scott Key penned the *Star Spangled Banner*). The two were married on May 8th, 1816, by a Lutheran pastor. Himself a single child, Hopkins would have fourteen children with Melusina in a marriage by all accounts as strong and blissful as his own parents' had been tenuous and tumultuous.

Hopkins traced his conversion to this time frame as well. One evening in the Winter of 1814-1815, while reading to himself, as "he often described it, a sudden beam of divine Truth shone into his inmost heart."[4] He experienced a "deep repentance, sincere humility, and loving faith," one centered upon "Christ crucified."[5] As with most endeavors in his life, Hopkins jumped into his newfound faith with gusto. Since no organized church existed in the area, he began holding Sunday services at his home for his workmen. In these services, he would use prayers from the Prayer Book, read Scripture, rehearse sermons that he could find, and add his own, brief exhortations.[6] Hopkins, however, was not committed to the Protestant Episcopal Church, having affinity in some ways to Presbyterianism, Quakerism, and even, early on, toward the Swedenborgians.

Shortly before marriage, Hopkins finally began studying for a career shift into the practice of law. The ore business had not proven as profitable or sustainable as advertised with decreasing market value and increasing debts. In fact, even with gracious help from a rich financier, Hopkins would walk away with significant financial loss from this career attempt. Also, Hopkins' interest in legal matters was revived and increased by his serving as a witness one day in the local courthouse. This experience confirmed in himself a love for legal argument and for logical reasoning. Hopkins began studying William Blackstone, the famous

[4] Hopkins, Jr., 43.
[5] *Ibid.*
[6] *Ibid.*, 44.

English jurist, in the evenings with the quizzing aid of his wife.[7] He then received admission to the Bar in April of 1818.[8] Upon this achievement, he began practicing in Pittsburgh and quickly gained a high reputation in the courtroom and financial stability for his home.

During this time, Hopkins and his family attended a Presbyterian church in Pittsburgh. He did so not, his son wrote, because of deep principle but more from friendly connections and the influential status of that tradition in his social and work circles. However, the rector of the local Episcopal parish, Trinity Church, asked him to play organ on Sundays. He agreed and, with his family joining him, all soon became convinced of the superiority of Prayer Book worship.[9]

The parish was small and remote from other Episcopal churches and struggled along rather than thrived. For a period of several years, from 1818-1823, a series of rectors served it but never for long. During this time, Hopkins sensed an inclination toward Holy Orders, but was unsure if he should pursue it due in part to the enjoyment and security his legal work provided. In the late Summer of 1823, shortly after the departure of one rector, a vestryman held a parish meeting without Hopkins' attendance or knowledge. There, the vestryman urged and obtained a vote to designate Hopkins the future rector of the parish. This designation assumed that Hopkins would give up the law and enter Holy Orders while serving the parish as lay reader until ordination. After some consideration, Hopkins accepted and the plan was agreed to by Bishop White. Hopkins immediately served the parish as lay reader, then received ordination to the diaconate on December 14th of that year and to the priesthood on May 12th of 1824.[10] The timing was extraordinarily quick and the election to serve a particular parish before ordination highly unusual. But the local needs, combined with Hopkins'

---

[7] Blackstone's *Commentaries on the Laws of England*, published in 1765, comprised the foundation for most lawyers' training throughout the 19th century, including Abraham Lincoln. See Albert W. Alschuler, "Rediscovering Blackstone," in *University of Pennsylvania Law Review* 145(1)(Nov. 1996): 2.
[8] Hopkins, Jr., 53.
[9] Ibid., 61-62.
[10] Ibid., 66-67.

own abilities and theological acumen, overcame concerns on this front from Bishop White.

Hopkins had a challenge on his hands. He began serving a church with only about 40 communicant members. Moreover, Trinity had basically no active sister parishes West of the Allegheny Mountains. Again throwing himself into the new endeavor, he acted with great energy to solidify and expand the parish. He helped to design a new church building, fashioning it in the style of the Gothic Revival then taking hold. His efforts won him applications from other parishes around the country asking for "Church plans" similar to his design for Trinity Church.[11] His love for designing church buildings resulted in the publication of his *Essay on Gothic Architecture* in 1836.[12] This composition included drawings and definitions of technical terms. It also provided a defense of physical beauty in the construction and decoration of worship space. It aided in the revival of the Gothic style that continues to exert significant influence in Episcopal church design today.

Hopkins also composed music for use in the parish which his wife played on the Church's organ. This was the same organ he had manned when first attending Trinity. He also aided the diocese, helping to found seven new churches in the region and thus being known, so his son recounted, as the father of the Diocese of Pittsburgh.[13]

Hopkins served Trinity Church as rector for eight years.[14] Yet news of his abilities and success spread beyond his region. Hopkins thus received a number of calls to minister to parishes in New York, all of which he declined. But he eventually did accept a call as an assistant rector at Trinity Church in Boston. George Washington Doane, later Bishop of New Jersey, had recently arrived as rector at the same parish. Hopkins made this move in hopes of realizing a growing dream: establishing a seminary based in his own diocese. His efforts to do so in

---

[11] *Ibid.*, 73.
[12] John Henry Hopkins, *Essay on Gothic Architecture* (Burlington, VT: Smith & Harrington, 1836).
[13] *Ibid.*, 75.
[14] Bentley Manning, "The Rt. Rev. John Henry Hopkins: a Compromising Catholicity" *Sewanee Theological Review* 58(2) (Spring 2015): 348.

Pittsburgh had met a cold response. In discussing a move to the Diocese of Massachusetts, he was given confidence that the plan would receive significant backing. Here Hopkins was disappointed again. A theological seminary was initiated in Boston with a promising start. Yet it very soon gave way to friction between Hopkins and Doane as well as failure to take the needed steps to establish the institution on a proper and lasting footing.[15]

After only a year in Boston, in 1832, the newly-formed Diocese of Vermont selected Hopkins as its first bishop. Already frustrated by the faltering of his hopes in Boston, Hopkins eventually accepted. In so accepting, he also took charge of a parish in the city of Burlington: St. Paul's. Vermont already was a challenging field for Episcopal ministry and would prove to be for the entirety of Hopkins more than three-decade bishopric. It was cut from the broader Eastern Diocese, which Bishop Alexander Viets Griswold had pastored since 1811. The new diocese did not have an extensive or deeply grounded Episcopal Church presence. The state and its parishes saw very slow numerical growth in part due to significant emigration by its inhabitants to more Western locations. Hopkins struggled throughout his long bishopric to bolster the diocese, including new attempts to establish institutions for his continued dream: in-house education for ministerial training. These efforts proved largely ineffective with some endeavors causing great pecuniary loss to Hopkins personally. They also revealed in Hopkins a zeal for ministry that was not fully accompanied with an acumen for business, finance, or administration.

In response, Hopkins' efforts and significant contributions turned toward the broader Protestant Episcopal Church. On this front he did see notable and lasting success. His training in the law especially aided the broader church. He helped usher through reforms to the trial of bishops, for instance.[16] These reforms came out of concrete experience. The 1840s and 1850s included the drama of three presentments

---

[15] Hopkins, Jr., 139-141.
[16] *Ibid.*, 217-219.

of formal charges brought against fellow bishops. These presentments resulted in the suspensions of Benjamin Onerdonk (of New York) and his brother, Henry (of Pennsylvania) for improper advances toward women and misuse of alcohol, respectively. Hopkins also participated in considering a presentment against his old ministry partner, now-Bishop Doane (New Jersey). This presentment involved charges of mishandling funds, a charge eventually dismissed. These were painful episodes in the Protestant Episcopal Church and partook of broader conflicts about theology and worship going on at the time. Apart from the merits of individual cases, Hopkins' work sought to give more procedural structure and clarity for such difficult moments in the life of the church.

The broader context of these presentments concerned the debates swirling between the High and Low Church parties within the Protestant Episcopal Church as well as the reaction to the influence of the Oxford Movement in America. He considered himself a member of the High Church party as compared to the Evangelical Low Church contingent, consistently siding with the former on questions related to the importance of episcopal government [17] and that party's reticence to participate in ecumenical organizations or to engage in extra-liturgical meetings.

Hopkins also expressed significant agreement with the Oxford Movement, meeting with some of its most important figures when in England. Early on, he praised what he saw as its return to a churchmanship more aligned with the Ancient Fathers. He at first even defended Newman's Tract 90 as a largely legitimate exposition of the Thirty-Nine Articles and as still distinctly Protestant in its grounding. Yet the growing defections to Rome in the early to mid-1840s soon roused Hopkins to greater criticism. By 1846, he gave a much harsher critique of Samuel Seabury, grandson of the original bishop of Connecticut, for his attempt to defend Tract 90's claims of the conformity of the Thirty-Nine Articles

---

[17] John Henry Hopkins, *Episcopal Government: A Sermon Preached at the Consecration of the Rev. Alonzo Potter* (Philadelphia: King & Baird, 1845).

to the Council of Trent.[18] Around the same time, he had a rancorous exchange with William Henry Hoyt, priest and rector at St. Luke's Church in St. Alban's, Vermont, regarding whether he had attended and participated in a Roman mass in the town. Hoyt gave evasive and argumentative responses. Against them, Hopkins asserted not only his episcopal authority but also defended the Protestant Episcopal Church and distinguished it from Roman Catholicism in an unsparing fashion.[19]

Thus, Hopkins believed that the Protestant in the name Protestant Episcopal Church was a feature, not a bug. Beyond his published letters to Hoyt, he composed several works further distinguishing the Episcopalian church from Roman Catholicism. In twin books, for example, Bishop Hopkins compared both 19th century Roman Catholicism and Episcopalianism to the early Church, arguing for the latter's greater fidelity to the Fathers.[20] These writings engaged not only with Scripture and Reformation history but showed his deep learning about the Early Church. He also published a series of lectures he gave on the English Reformation, defending that period as a return to how the Father's approached Scripture, tradition, and a number of particular doctrines reclaimed at that time.[21]

However, Hopkins was disposed to recognize a broad tent within Christianity in general and the Protestant Episcopal Church in particular. When in England in the 1830s, he did not just meet with the Tractarians but also those Low-Church Evangelicals then arguing against them. His wide latitude came out in several writings. For one, in November of 1849, he published an address to the clergy in his diocese

[18] Hopkins, Jr., 234. See also Hopkins, *Reply to the Letter of Dr. Seabury* (New York: John R. Wisner, 1846).

[19] John Henry Hopkins, *Pastoral Letter, Addressed by the Bishop of the Protestant Episcopal Church in the State of Vermont, to the People of His Diocese, on the Subject of His Correspondence with the Rev. William Henry Hoyt* (Burlington: Chauncy Goodrich, 1846).

[20] See *The Primitive Church Compared with the Protestant Episcopal Church* (Burlington, VT: Smith and Harrison, 1835); *The Church of Rome in Her Primitive Purity, Compared with the Church of Rome at the Present Day* (London: J.G. & F. Rivington, 1839).

[21] John Henry Hopkins, *Sixteen Lectures on the Causes, Principles, and Results of the British Reformation* (Philadelphia: James M. Campbell, 1844).

on the Gorham Controversy then taking place within the Church of England. In 1847, Gorham was denied a post by Bishop Henry Philpotts because Gorham held to a "Calvinistic" view of infant baptism, denying that internal, spiritual regeneration automatically accompanied the rite. Gorham objected that his view not only was an acceptable one according to the Church of England's standards but was the one held by most if not all the composers of the Church's formularies. Hopkins wrote after the ecclesiastical Court of Arches affirmed Philpotts' decision but before the governmental Judicial Committee of the Privy Council overturned it. Hopkins sided with Gorham. He did so not because he fully agreed with Gorham's position on baptism but because he believed it irrefutable that the presbyter's perspective rested squarely within the acceptable range of views on the matter within the Church of England and her daughter churches. Though disclaiming being a Calvinist, Hopkins freely admitted, with supporting evidence, that such views dominated the Church of England at least until the reign of Charles I and, though no longer a majority, still was a position held by a significant number of clergy in England and the United States.

On the other hand, Hopkins defended more ornate modes of worship, even when those modes did not agree with his own practice. In making this point, Bishop Hopkins published *The Law of Ritualism* in 1866, two years before his death.[22] Many at the time, especially in the Evangelical camp, saw the growing fondness for rituals in liturgical dress and the decoration of worship space as a clear slide toward Rome. In response, Hopkins declared that he would base his argument in favor of ritual on Protestant grounds, referring to his decades of defending the Reformation against Rome and defining the Episcopal Church as a Protestant body.

Hopkins first defended ritualism through a Biblical theology that emphasized continuity in worship practices between the Old and New Testament Church. Jewish persons, in fact, were still bound by Old

---

[22] John Henry Hopkins, *The Law of Ritualism* (New York: Hurd & Houghton, 1866).

Testament rites except for the sacrifices and the Aaronic priesthood, both of which Christ fulfilled to the point of abrogating.[23] To these the Jews must add the sacraments instituted by Jesus—Baptism and Holy Communion. Gentiles were free from obligation to follow the Old Testament ceremonials. However, Hopkins argued they had the freedom to appropriate those rites and that the Early Church did so on many fronts, decisions which should receive significant deference from the Church today. Hopkins went on to defend the legitimacy (though not the requirement) to use incense and certain vestments, to refer to the Table or the Altar, and other acts gaining prominence in the Ritualist movement. As noted before, Hopkins correctly predicted these changes would become the majority practice.

Finally, in answer to the claim that these rituals confused the Church of England and the Protestant Episcopal Church with Rome, Hopkins answered that the Reformation sought to correct false doctrine, not change ceremonial practice. He even gave a long list of doctrinal errors that he claimed undergirded the Reformation and that continued within Roman Catholicism. These included that church's views on the papacy, "the worship of the virgin Mary and the Saints,"[24] clerical celibacy, private confession, purgatory, and the relationship of Scripture to tradition.[25] The linking of the growing ritualism to these false doctrines was illegitimate in Hopkins' view and he denied the equation vehemently. The worship practices of ritualism were a return to the Early Church, not dressing up to swim the Tiber.

In addition to these theological debates, Hopkins' legal mind never left him. Along these lines, the Bishop published a work on politics, both about its theory and its manifestation under the United States Constitution. There, he argued that America's Constitution was Christian and, through its oath requirements, demanded only Christian officeholders. He also discussed the relationship between politics and other social institutions such as the family. His view of religious liberty

---

[23] Hopkins, *Ritualism*, 9-15.
[24] *Ibid.*, 52.
[25] *Ibid.*, 51-57, 95.

PART III: INTELLECTUALS

included wide protections for Christians (including Roman Catholics) and Jews, but permitted, even demanded, suppression of all other religious (and non-religious) expressions, actions, and institutions.[26]

Regarding politics, the American Civil War dominated the latter years of his life and bishopric. Undoubtedly the most controversial of Hopkins writings for today consisted of several works discussing American chattel slavery that he published in the lead up to and during the War. In them, he expressed personal hope for eventual emancipation as well as arguing the institution enabled, even encouraged certain sinful activity. Yet he vigorously defended the institution as in accordance with Scripture and thus not inherently evil.[27] Emancipation would be a matter of prudence, not moral necessity.

He also protested against the 1862 letter from the House of Bishops, composed by Bishop Charles McIlvaine of Ohio, condemning the clergy in the Southern states for supporting secession efforts. Hopkins thought the church should not comment on civil matters as it did here.[28] Bishop Hopkins then proved essential in bringing the Southern bishops fully back into the Protestant Episcopal Church, beginning with the General Convention in Philadelphia in October of 1865, only a few months after the cessation of hostilities.[29] At this time, Hopkins took the place of Presiding Bishop, a position reserved to the longest-tenured bishop within the church. The bishop also attended the first Lambeth Conference in 1867[30] where he preached a sermon and participated in its deliberations. He gave his last sermon not long thereafter, on December

[26] John Henry Hopkins, *The American Citizen: His Rights and Duties According to the Spirit of the Constitution of the United States* (New York: Pudney and Russell, 1857).
[27] John Henry Hopkins, *The American Citizen*, 121-165; *A Scriptural, Ecclesiastical, and Historical View of Slavery* (New York: W.I. Pooley & Co., 1864); Donald, 75-76.
[28] Perry, 2: 336.
[29] James M. Donald, "Bishop Hopkins and the Reunification of the Church" in *Historical Magazine of the Protestant Episcopal Church* 47(1)(March 1978): 73-75.
[30] Hopkins, III, 276.

1, 1867, at his home parish of St. Paul's. He died just a little over a month later, on January 9, 1868.

We can see in Hopkins much that translates to the American Episcopal tradition in the Twenty-first Century. For, although little known today, Bishop Hopkins charted a course that many now take. This course seeks to combine doctrinal, liturgical, and ecclesiastical principles from within the broad tent of the Anglican Communion. If such a vision is to work today, its adherents would do well to look to Bishop Hopkins as a model.

William Meade
1789-1862

Bishop William Meade of Virginia slept restlessly on the night of January 3rd, 1861. Two weeks earlier a specially called convention in South Carolina passed a secession resolution severing the ties of that state with the United States of America. The Bishop had throughout his life maintained a conservative posture in almost every aspect of his ministry, his politics, and his social dispositions. This meant that unlike the fire-eater, pro-slavery intellectuals and politicians, William Meade saw himself as an unambiguous union man. He feared that secession inevitably led to war, and that war led to destruction, and that all of the chaos that potentially might come from a sectional crisis between free and slave states would be God's righteous judgment passed on an unrighteous people. The prominence of the office of Bishop of Virginia gave him considerable social influence during the sectional crisis. His celebrity gained him access to powerful men in Washington City, the federal capital. He wrote letters to politicians he knew, and he wrote letters to northern brother bishops. Not a man known for his emotions, Meade proved to be surprisingly emotional as he unburdened himself to Ohio bishop Charles P. McIlvaine over the potential breakup of the American republic. "If the ministers of the Prince of Peace can do nothing in the interest of peace, how can we expect the selfish politicians to do it? I am almost in despair. I have put forth a form of prayer for the present crisis." He prayed daily and urged the governor of Virginia to call a day of fasting or at least prayer to no avail. Meade took it upon himself to call a day of fasting, and he urged his priests to pray for a peaceful resolution to the political conflict that threatened to quickly become violent. He held out hope nonetheless for peace and told Bishop McIlvaine, "I believe that good sense, self-interest, and religion, with God's providence, will arrest the calamity of disunion."

The Meade family always enjoyed good standing in colonial Virginia Society. When the American revolution came, they, like many other gentry families, joined the cause of the patriots. The future bishop's father, Richard Kidder Meade, served in the Continental Army as a colonel. Colonel Meade came to the notice of the army's commanding general, George Washington. General Washington placed Meade on his staff, undoubtedly, because Colonel Meade proved himself to be a confident soldier, but it is also likely that Washington wanted to be surrounded by men like him. While not of the first rank of the Virginia aristocracy, the Meades like Washington were comfortably gentry. Meade's mother, Mary, married into the Randolph family and was widowed before marrying Richard Meade in 1780. Colonel Meade's standing in society was such that he could prevail upon a woman who had been a part of one of the First Family's of Virginia—colloquially called the FFVs—to marry him. Meade owned a sizable plantation straddling what is now modern Chesterfield and Henrico counties with enough enslaved human beings to qualify for the planter class. William Meade's unionism, and his paradoxical comfort with human bondage and emancipationist reforms, all represented the normal dispositions of the Revolutionary era of Virginians. The new American republic in many ways influenced the religious beliefs of the new republican citizenry in Virginia more than churches did. Thomas Jefferson and his dissenter Evangelical allies—particularly Baptists, Methodists, and Presbyterians—saw the newly independent states as a religious *tabula rasa* that could be transformed into a laboratory for true religious freedom. It was in Virginia, they believed, that the fight for religious liberty needed to take place, not simply because there were a significant number of dissenter allies for Jefferson's cause—there were—but also because it was in Virginia that the Anglican establishment had its most powerful and well-placed allies. When Meade was born in November of 1789, he was born into a society that religious historian Martin E. Marty argued was the first society to move away from the Constantinian order that had defined Western Christianity for over 1,400 years. The Meades, however, along with many aristocratic families in Virginia, gave only qualified support to Jefferson's new religious regime, and for good reason. Jeffersonian enthusiasts accused Anglican rectors of being closeted loyalists and probable traitors. Priests known to have harbored sympathies for the king were victims of violence, and on at least one occasion an Anglican minister was shot at.[1]

The legacy of Jefferson never sat easily with Virginia Episcopalians. Most felt comfortable with disestablishment—Bishop James Madison, cousin of the fourth president of the United States, publicly extolled disestablishment—but that did not mean Church of England-turned-Episcopal Virginians supported the broader Jeffersonian disposition to remove religion's influence from the civil, cultural, and political spheres. Religion's role in education, for example, remained of paramount importance for gentry Virginians and Richard Kidder Meade insisted that his son be tutored by a local Anglican priest near their sizable manor house in modern-day Clarke County, Virginia. The school met at Carter Hall, the home of a local notable, and was run by a Rev. Mr. Wiley, who "abstained from the exercises" of the sacred functions of the priesthood "and devoted himself to secular teaching." Local grandees held Wiley in high regard as a scholar and a teacher. He was "well qualified," and pursued teaching "with great enthusiasm and singular success." Bishop John Johns, Meade's first major biographer and

---

[1] Philip Slaughter, *Memoir of the Life of the Rt. Rev. William Meade, D. D., Bishop of the Diocese of Virginia* (John Wilson and Son, 1885), 7-8; Martin E. Marty, "The Virginia Statute Two Hundred Years Later," in Merrill D. Peterson and Robert Vaughan eds., *The Virginia Statute for Religious Freedom: Its Evolution and Consequences in American History* (Cambridge and. New York: Cambridge University Press, 1988), 3; Thomas B. Allen, *1789: George Washington and the Founders Create America* (Lanham, MD: Rowman & Littlefield, 2023), 124.

his successor as Bishop of Virginia, noted that Wiley's "reputation as a classical teacher was not confined to Carter Hall. In the course of a few years he was elected principal of a flourishing academy in Fredericktown, Maryland, and afterwards professor of languages in St. John's College, Annapolis, where he remained till his death." William Meade became a student of Wiley's at age ten, and flourished under the latter's tutelage. Meade's "literary taste, and more especially his fondness for the ancient classics, were skillfully cultivated by the intelligence and zeal of Mr. Wiley. The happy effect of this training was soon apparent in the successful collegiate course of the pupil." Meade's vision of education and his vision of ministry routinely wedded the Christian scriptures, the Classics, and moral philosophy. Meade's opus, aptly titled *The Bible and the Classics* and published the year before his death, exemplified Meade's lifelong commitment to the church and education, as well as his ecclesiastical and intellectual conservatism.

Carter Hall gave Meade a good intellectual and social foundation. With Rev. Wiley he gained erudition and he flourished socially as well. Meade's athleticism and competitive drive pushed him to excel in sports. His athletic prowess, coupled with an innate social confidence, made him a popular schoolmate and a prominent potential suitor for young women from the local aristocracy. This same confidence later typified Meade's interactions with peer bishops.

By age seventeen Meade, with two fellow schoolmates, entered the College of New Jersey. They arrived at what is now Princeton University in the Fall of 1806. Four years earlier a fire wrecked the campus and Princeton was engaged in a process of rebuilding its physical plant and reformulating the curriculum. The leading intellectual influence on the campus at the end of the Eighteenth and beginning of the Nineteenth centuries was President Samuel Stanhope Smith, and the college he oversaw emphasized Scottish Common Sense realism as its guiding intellectual philosophy. Common Sense philosophy was a Scot Presbyterian articulation of natural law, wherein all humans—common meaning universal—had a sense of what was naturally true because of their human nature. When Meade arrived in 1806, the college was perhaps the most intellectually and socially conservative institution of higher learning outside of New England. That conservative disposition attracted a mix of Scotch-Irish Presbyterians interested in preparing for ministry, and aristocratic youths particularly from the southern states. Pre-seminary education became less of a priority for Princeton as the first decade of the nineteenth century wore on, and students from Episcopal backgrounds formed a larger part of the student body. Meade as a student conspicuously engaged in the fraternal activities of the student body, which included regular visits to taverns and social dancing. The college student Meade was very different than the future bishop who advised communicants against social dancing and tavern-going. When the administration disciplined a group of students for behaving in ungentlemanly and un-Christian ways, Meade sided with his fellow students. [2]

Samuel Stanhope Smith did not conceal his dislike of what he perceived as rising atheism and freethinking, particularly in the Southern states. Meade's family's politics and religiosity likewise never embraced the Jeffersonian dispositions so celebrated in the aftermath of the American revolution. In his later years Meade said that he saw the religious revolution that Virginia underwent as a sort of unchurching, wherein Evangelical churches tore down older institutional aspects of Protestant life. [3]

Unlike other churchmen of the era, Meade never spoke of a specific conversion experience. He indicated that his family had been pious and that he never knew a time he did not believe he was a Christian. Meade's biographer Philip Slaughter wrote that "religion was the primary thing in Bishop Meade, the ruling force which determined his

---

[2] John Johns, *A Memoir of the Life of the Right Rev. William Meade, D.D., Bishop of the Protestant Episcopal Church in the Diocese of Virginia* (Baltimore: Innes, 1867), 15.

[3] Mark A. Noll, *Princeton and the Republic, 1768-1822: The Search for a Christian Enlightenment in the Era of Samuel Stanhope Smith* (Princeton, NJ: Princeton University Press, 1989), 164-65; William Meade, *Old Churches, Ministers, and Families of Virginia Vol. 1* (Philadelphia, PA: J.P. Lippincott and Co., 1872), 24.

character and career." The seed of his lifelong faith "had been planted in the virgin soil of his infant heart, and its first germinations had been watched by the loving eye, watered by the tears, and tended by the skilled hand of his mother, who habitually looked to God 'to give the increase.'" Meade "did not remember a time when he did not 'think himself a subject of the operations of the Holy Spirit.'" His college years were not marked by the same type of piety that typified his childhood, but Meade still regularly attended divine service as a young man. Nonetheless the future bishop felt guilty over his college years. "His mother was not there to call him to prayer, and pray with him. Boys have their law of honor, which does not often coincide with the law of God; what the boys think and say and do is the law of their miniature republics. Under these influences his spiritual growth was dwarfed, if not arrested." Still, Meade's religiosity stayed with him. Socially, he disliked the fervor of both dissenter Evangelicals and freethinkers that influenced Virginia in the late Eighteenth and early Nineteenth Centuries. [4]

Princeton confirmed what would prove to be a lifelong conservative disposition in William Meade. Class undoubtedly formed Meade intellectually and socially, and contributed to his conservatism. While not of the first rank of Virginia families, the Meades earned the respect of the Commonwealth's high aristocrats. Young William mixed with the family of the late President Washington, and his social circle brought him into contact with Mary Nelson, granddaughter of a former governor of Virginia. Meade and Mary married in January 1810. Marriage undoubtedly made the sporty youth more serious. Meade's transformation into the grave bishop he was in later years can be traced not only to his marriage, but also to an chronic illness he developed at the end of his time in Princeton. The illness affected his eyesight. Meade also endured a near-fatal illness the same year. His marriage into the upper echelons of the state aristocracy, combined with significant struggles with health, reoriented Meade away from socializing and towards

---

[4] Slaughter, *Memoir*, 10-11; Johns, *A Memoir of the Life of the Right Rev. William Meade*, 17-18

the Christian ministry, which he decided to pursue as a vocation while at Princeton. His subsequent conservatism as a bishop stemmed from his own self-conception that he was not merely a conservative but a sort of counterrevolutionary against the Enlightenment in Virginia. Meade believed that the Virginia of his childhood was a hotbed of "infidelity" and what he called "French"—then a euphemism for atheism and freethinking —"politics and religion." Every educated young man, he complained, could be expected to be "a skeptic, if not an avowed unbeliever."

As a priest and later as a bishop, Meade was determined to whip piety back into Virginia. His future subordinate priests noted that he did not fail to use the "rod" to do so. When Bishop James Madison ordained Meade in February 1811, one commentator joked that the icy Blue Ridge Mountain weather matched the bishop's ministry. Undeniably, Meade's personality lacked the jovial bonhomie that his immediate predecessors James Madison and Richard Channing Moore had in abundance. His intensity and his preaching, however, made him a popular minister in the parishes he led. Unlike many of the incumbents in the priesthood, Meade also exhibited energy in diocesan matters that made him indispensable in particular to Bishop Moore, who never enjoyed robust health. Meade served as an assistant to Alexander Balmain at the congregation in Frederick County until 1821, when Meade became the primary priest. A number of curates served under him assisting burgeoning mission churches in Frederick, Clark, and Shenandoah counties. Meade traveled widely himself and gained a reputation as a passionate preacher. Connections with Virginia's political class allowed Meade to be a more effective fundraiser than the diocese had previously. Meade, for example, successfully petitioned John Marshall to help fund the then infant theological seminary in the state. Meade's family history, his own conservative political preferences, and the fact that he was raised an Anglican wedded his ministry to a traditional understanding of Anglican liturgy and theology. In the beginning of the Nineteenth Century, that meant what might be today defined as Old High Church or Evangelical High Church, although neither term would have made much sense to Meade. What was clear is that Meade saw the Tractarian movement and certain

High Church innovations as progressive and indicative of a departure from the English Reformation. For Meade and older Episcopal families, the essential point of separation they affirmed from other magisterial Protestants was not sacramental but ecclesiological. Bishops defined the true church, more than a specific sacramentology or philosophy of history did. The Evangelical party in Early Republic Virginia represented liturgical and social conservatism more than Tractarian sympathizers did. Bishop Ravenscroft and New England hyper-Calvinist born Bishop Ives, both who governed the diocese of North Carolina in succession, for example, hailed from middle class backgrounds and both underwent radical and often unstable liturgical transformations in revivalist contexts before becoming Episcopalians. And both disliked conservative Evangelical and patrician Meade. Meade's relationship to broad church Bishop Moore was not intimate, but they were cordial and Moore saw Meade's talents. Evangelicals and conservatives in Virginia adored Meade, and so when Moore asked for an assistant bishop in 1832, Meade was the logical choice, even if he grated on some High Churchmen. Ravenscroft refused to attend Meade's consecration. Bishop Ives later converted to Roman Catholicism, which Meade saw as a vindication of his dislike of Tractarianism. Later confrontations with Bishop Onderdonk of New York and Bishop Doane of New Jersey reinforced the idea among High Churchmen that Meade was nothing more than narrow-minded and haughty patrician, while rumors of Doane's financial shenanigans and Onderdonk's alleged immorality convinced Meade that Tractarianism was nothing more than antinomian charlatanism.[5]

Consecration in 1832 made Meade a bishop, but he deferred to the diocesan ordinary, Richard Channing Moore, until the latter's death

---

[5] Johns, *A Memoir*, 54; T.G. Dashiel, "History of the Church in Virginia to the Death of Bishop Meade" in *Addresses and Historical Papers Before the Centennial Council of the Protestant Episcopal Church in Virginia* (New York: Thomas Whitaker, 1885), 66-67; Lewis Wright, "Anglo-Catholocism in Antebellum North Carolina: Levi Silliman Ives and the Society of the Holy Cross." *Anglican and Episcopal History* 69, no. 1 (2000): 44–71; William Meade, *Statement of Bishop Meade in Reply to Some Parts of Bishop Onderdonk's Statement* (New York: Stanford and Sword, 1845).

and Meade's elevation in 1841. He appeared to some of his parishioners—accustomed to the days of Georgian moral laxity—as a grave, albeit earnest, religious aesthete. The Episcopal church historian charged with writing Meade's official church biography in 1885 noted that regarding "discipline in the diocese, Mr. Meade had from the beginning preached a crusade against horse-racing, card-playing, the theatre, and such like fashionable amusements, as inconsistent with a Christian profession." Meade denounced perceived unchurchly activities in public, and followed his public statements up "with private admonitions in person, and by reasonings, remonstrance, affectionate entreaties, and by letters unknown to all but himself and the persons addressed." Meade "knew the State well, and had seen the desolation wrought in families, and in society." As a younger man he saw what historian Susan Dunn in her *Dominion of Memories* termed as the wholesale economic and social collapse of Virginia between 1800 and 1830. Former United States president James Madison Jr. remarked that his home state came upon "hard times" after the War of 1812. Monticello appeared to postmaster general William Barry in 1832 as an example of "dilapidation and ruin." Mount Vernon had to one visitor "an aspect of forlorn neediness." [6]

    Meade saw ecclesiastical disorder and consequently spiritual weakness as a primary reason for Virginia's socio-economic collapse. "For about two hundred years did the Episcopal Church of Virginia try the experiment of a system, whose constitution required such an head, but was actually without it." No bishop came to Virginia, "as the Church requires, to watch over the conduct, and punish the vices of the Clergy; none to administer the rite of Confirmation, and thus admit the faithful to the Supper of the Lord." Meade stated his support for the episcopacy by noting that "it must be evident, that the Episcopal Church without such an officer is more likely to suffer for the want of Godly discipline, than any other society of Christians, because all others have some substitute, whereas our own Church makes this office indispensable to some

---

[6] Susan Dunn, *Dominion of Memories: Jefferson, Madison, and the Decline of Virginia* (New York: Basic Books, 2007), 6-8.

important parts of ecclesiastical government and discipline." A church without a bishop became a corrupt and lax church, and Meade believed the church in Virginia had been sullied by its lack of a bishop. "Such being the corrupt state of the Church in Virginia, it is not wonderful that here, as in England, disaffection should take place and dissent begin." Meade "enumerated several counties in which costly mansions, where an elegant hospitality had been dispensed, had lapsed into the hands of strangers, and broad acres which had waved with golden grain were now overgrown with cedar and pine, the evergreen memorials of Virginia's prodigal sons." As bishop, "he never ceased this crusade until, after angry opposition in many conventions, his views were embodied in the nineteenth canon of discipline, and in the canon disqualifying non-communicants for being deputies in convention." He emphasized family prayer because he believed it was a chief "thermometer of the religious temperature of the heads of houses." He made catechesis more robust and was far stricter on who communed than either of his predecessors. He wanted to, in the words of Bishop Johns, reform the font and the pulpit. Meade was no moralist, however, and he urged parishioners to confront the fact that their morality could not save them; Christ, not virtue, was the way of salvation.[7]

Governing a diocese in the largest slave state and with the single largest number of slaveholders meant that chattel slavery remained a constant reality in the bishop's life and in the lives of those he shepherded. Meade, like the vast majority of southern churchmen, did not endorse religious opposition to slavery on political grounds. Meade's innate conservatism revolted at calls from Episcopalians like John Jay—grandson of the first chief justice—who wanted a holy war against slavery spearheaded by the church hierarchy. Meade emancipated his own slaves and separated from most southern ministers by his willingness

[7] William Meade, *A Brief Review of the Episcopal Church in Virginia, From its First Establishment to its Present Time* (Richmond, VA: William McFarland, 1845), 4-5; Slaughter, *Memoir of the Life of the Rt. Rev. William Meade*, 17-18; Johns, *A Memoir*, 61 Eugene Genovese and Elizabeth Fox-Genovese, *The Mind of the Master Class: History and Faith in the Southern Slaveholders' Worldview* (Cambridge: Cambridge University Press, 2005), 529.

to preach sermons centered on biblical affirmations of emancipation. As a young presbyter who regularly preached in Alexandria, Meade earned a reputation as a moderate on the issue of slavery. His churchmanship placed him firmly in the Evangelical wing of the Episcopal Church, which entertained emancipation and colonization as possible resolutions to what was increasingly viewed as the problem of slavery's maintenance in Virginia. Francis Scott Key, a leading proponent of the American Colonization Society often listened to Meade, and he praised the young rector's preaching. John Randolph of Roanoke, the eccentric Virginia representative and senator, attended sermons by Meade as well. Randolph's rejection of his former freethinking and flirtation with Islam in 1818 led to regular churchgoing. Meade's evangelical pastoral tone and association of the Christian life with freedom served as part of Randolph's motivation to free his slaves at the end of his life. Meade never held much enthusiasm for perpetuating slavery. In 1819 he traveled to Georgia to procure legal assistance for "for the release of recaptured Africans who were about to be sold; and succeeded in his mission. In going to and returning from the South, he was active in establishing auxiliaries to the American Colonization Society, and prosecuted his mission through the Middle to the New England States." Meade's biographers noted that the future bishop "did not believe the holding of slaves, in the circumstances of the South, to be a sin; but he maintained it to be the paramount duty of masters to give their negroes religious instruction. He emancipated his own slaves; but this experiment proved so disastrous to the negroes that he ceased to encourage it." In 1833, when John Randolph died after providing for the sensational emancipation of his three hundred slaves, Meade served as an executor to Randolph's will. More important for his ministry as a bishop, Meade wrote a pastoral letter urging slaveholders to catechize the enslaved people on their plantations. Meade's letter is important because he broke with southern politicians who warned about the dangers of teaching slaves to read. Meade was no progressive on slavery, but he was committed enough to the church to disregard fears of slaves reading. The Bible was more important than southern civil law. [8]

While slavery undoubtedly was a political issue during his episcopacy, Meade never preached partisan sermons. Like most Virginians of his era he disliked the symbiosis that wedded the Federalist Party and New England's state churches, and he supported disestablishment like his prelate predecessors had. But he was not a churchman who hid his politics from presbyters or the laity. Robert Nelson, a priest under Meade, wrote that the bishop was a strong government man, and a disciplinarian by education, temperament and faith." Strong government in the antebellum United States often indicated an affinity with the Whig Party, and it is likely that in as much as Meade was political, his broad sympathies were with the Whigs who saw a more expansive place for institutional religion in civic life and in politics than Andrew Jackson's Democrats did. Meade "held to the traditions of his forefathers and mothers on this point, as firmly as 'the pharisees held the traditions of the elders.' But he was not one like the pharisees to 'say and do not.'" Nelson related a story of how when the "Bishop was a boy, his spartan mother was one day 'not sparing the rod but chastening her son betimes,' when an aunt of his coming near, showed her appreciation of the performance by exclaiming, 'give it to him well.'" Meade, then, "trained, as he was, under such hands, and in schools and days when neither sentimentalism nor sensationalism, but solid truth and matter of fact were the order and spirit of the day," did not hesitate to discipline his flock in ways that approached what even his partisans saw as severity.

[8] John Jay, *Thoughts on the duty of the Episcopal Church, in relation to Slavery* (New York: Piercy & Reed, 1839), 5-7; Gregory May, *A Madman's Will: John Randolph, Four Hundred Slaves, and the Mirage of Freedom* (New York: Liverlight, 2023); Slaughter, *Memoir of the Life of the Rt. Rev. William Meade*, 17-18; Marc Leepson, *What so Proudly We Hailed: Francis Scott Key, a Life* (New York: Palgrave Macmillan, 2014), 144; William Meade, *Sermons Address to Masters and Servants, and Published in the Year 1743, by the Rev. Thomas Bacon, Minister of the Protestant Episcopal Church in Maryland, Now Republished with other Tracts and Dialogues on the Same Subject, and Recommended to all Masters and Mistresses to Be Used in Their Families* (Winchester, VA: John Heiskell, 1813).

Nelson nonetheless did not view Meade as a martinet. He was a representative man of his class and generation. "It is no wonder that with the fiber of which he was formed, this Bishop should never have grown to think that erring boys and girls no longer needed discipline at home and school, nor erring men and women, in the church."[9]

The most serious test of Meade's leadership proved to be his last. The secession crisis that swept across the South aligned Fire-Eater radicals against conservative unionists in Virginia, as well as the other southern states. Meade called disunion a calamity, and with Alabama Bishop Nicholas Cobb and Tennessee's James Hervey Otey, formed a phalanx of Unionists bishops who refused to budge on what they believed as the imprudence of secession. Meade's vision of the church in Virginia had been formed in the heady days of the new republic. So too had his politics. One Virginia lady believed that the same courtly disposition that drove Meade to govern his diocese with gravity and rigidity was what kept him from endorsing a political theory he thought of as innovative and dangerous. "The old gentleman" tried to hold the tide of secession at bay as long as he could, but he ultimately gave way when his home state seceded after Abraham Lincoln called for soldiers to quash the Confederacy and secession in April of 1861. Because of his seniority, he became the first presiding bishop of the Episcopal Church in the Confederate States, a role he neither relished nor wanted. His health had been failing for some time, and the travel of his new duties, despite not being particularly onerous, effectively killed him. Meade died on March 14, 1862. His legacy lived, however, in the form of a diocese in better educational, financial, liturgical, and sociological condition than it had ever been before. William Sparrow, a professor at the Protestant Episcopal Seminary in Alexandria, eulogized Meade and reminded his grieving listeners that Meade "lived to see the Church in Virginia 'in great prosperity.'" Never was it so prosperous as at the commencement

---

[9] Slaughter, *Memoir*, 12, Robert Nelson, *Reminiscences of the Rev. William Meade, Bishop of the Prot. Epis. Church in Virginia* (Shanghai, 1873), 13-14. Genovese and Fox-Genovese, *The Mind of the Master Class*, 478; Johns, *A Memoir*, 524-525.

of our national troubles." Meade gathered through the years "a body of parochial clergy, surpassed by none for faithfulness and efficiency as pastors. He saw the congregations committed to their care increasing yearly in all the fruits of the Spirit." Meade's ministry had international influence as well. "Missionary zeal was spreading on every hand, and substantial aid more and more afforded to the cause. Neither Foreign, Domestic, or Diocesan Missions were overlooked." His educational emphasis resulted in "the Education Society for the aid of young men preparing for the ministry." The Education Society had the distinction of "deriving an adequate support from Virginia alone, though helping young men from all the States." Other "educational institutions for both sexes, in connection with the Church, were prospering; and the Theological Seminary was far better provided with every species of accommodation, and better filled with students, than it ever had been before" Meade's ministry had been grave, but steady. "In the progress of things towards this point of prosperity, it should also be mentioned, there had been very little fluctuation, and no 'back-sets.' Owing to the consummate prudence of him who took a leading part in all these matters, the progress of the Diocese had been as continuous and unbroken, as the advance of the dawn to broad daylight."[10]

[10] Johns, *A Memoir*, 575

Conclusion

American Anglicanism spends much of its time discussing and debating its identity. We contain significant variety in our self-understanding and thus in our beliefs and practices. This variety includes healthy, balancing points of emphasis that have been with this tradition for centuries. But they also involve problematic tensions, perhaps even contradictions, which create tenuous unity in regular danger either of rupture or descent into chaos. What made the bishops of the Antebellum United States so influential in their own time, and what makes them useful to us in the early Twenty-First Century, is that despite their differences they managed to create and sustain a national Protestant church that operated with significant liturgical and theological unity even as they endured tensions that typified their era.

Despite innovations of the Tractarian movement, impaired communion during the Civil War, and the rapid social and cultural changes in the Nineteenth Century United States, Bishop Gregory T. Bedell of Ohio rightfully described the first century of the Episcopal Church as a narrative of substantive success and unity. From humble beginnings in 1785, the Episcopal Church grew in stature and in mission. "A little one," Bedell told a British audience in London's St. Paul's Cathderal, "has become a thousand, and a small one a strong nation." In a space of "only a hundred years" the Lord had hastened the Episcopal Church "in His time." Bedell, a prominent Evangelical, nonetheless reassured his listeners

CONCLUSION

that despite the Americanization and growth of Anglicanism in the North American republic, Episcopalians did not "forget our debt to the Church of England for its nurture." American bishops remembered their debts to the English Reformation and the the Church of England, so much so that it had "imbedded the fact in the opening sentences of the Preface to our Book of Common Prayer, and to all generations perpetuate the record, that 'to the Church of England the Protestant Episcopal Church in these States is indebted, under God, for her first foundation, and a long continuance of nursing care and protection.'" A short history of the Episcopal Church published for the laity reminded parishioners that bishops had as their calling "the unity of faith, doctrine, discipline, and uniformity of worship" in the Episcopal Church and with the mother churches in Great Britain. Unity and tradition wedded to still substantive theological conformity gave the Episcopal Church strength. Strength and unity came from prelates doing their jobs, and the laity looked to the bishops for good order, Protestant orthodoxy, and Prayer Book orthopraxy.[1]

Reflexive lay trust in bishops waned in the early Twentieth Century and ended altogether by the beginning of the new millennium. The vacuum left by episcopal theological heterodoxy and mismanagement led some laypeople to look for a variety of alternative authorities to guide Anglicanism in the new century. Some have looked to the Early Church for answers on the identity question. Others seek out some era of the Church of England, whether in its Edwardian, Elizabethan, Laudian, or Oxford iterations. Still others look, sometimes unknowingly, to the liturgical innovations that took place after Vatican II.

These sources offer varying levels of help in the search for an American Anglican identity. But one source has been sorely lacking

---

[1] Gregory T. Bedell, *The Centenary of the American Episcopacy* (London: The Society for the Propagation of the Gospel in Foreign Parts, 1884), 3; William Behman, *A Short History of the Episcopal Church in the United States* (New York, NY: E.P. Dutton and Co., 1884), 76-77.

CONCLUSION

in these discussions: the historic Protestant Episcopal Church. Though closest to us in geography and ecclesial history, we seem to know little about it, much less receive influence from it in our views of doctrine, liturgy, polity, and more. The Protestant Episcopal Church of the Nineteenth Century not only provides an important historic tradition for modern North American Anglicans; it also provides a tradition that effectively maintained relative unity amongst churchmen whose theological differences might have led to fracture of the Episcopal Church. That the fracture occurred at the beginning of the Twenty-First Century, and not in the era of the Tractarian movement, the Civil War, and en masse societal democratization is a testament to the strength of antebellum and broader Nineteenth Century Episcopal leadership.

The modern clerical and lay blind spot regarding the Early Republic episcopacy is to our detriment. However, we need not remain blind to our past. Interest in Anglican history is on the rise, and lay interest in Anglican history feeds a burgeoning historiography of what is generally rendered Anglicanism. All too often, however, works of Anglican history tend to skip the history of the Episcopal Church in the United States in the interest of finding an often contrived ancient pedigree for Anglican churchmanship in North America. This oversight has very real doctrinal, ecclesiastical, and sociological consequences for both the Episcopal Church and the Anglican Church in North America; few parishioners in either communion know what their leaders historically believed about the faith once received.

Bishops of the Protestant Episcopal Church in the United States in the antebellum era did in fact have firm beliefs regarding church tradition, ecclesiology, and liturgy. These beliefs were distinctively Anglican, distinctly ancient, and distinctly Reformational. On May 21st, 1851, the convention of the Virginia diocese of the Protestant Episcopal Church met in Staunton, located about forty miles west of Charlottesville. Bishop William Meade delivered an address to the gathering titled, "The True Churchman."[2] In those remarks, Bishop Meade articulated his understanding of the Protestant Episcopal Church. He defined his church in historical, doctrinal, and liturgical terms. Historically, Meade noted the Protestant Episcopal Church descended from the Early Church. But it did so with a particular genealogy. It first came from the Western church in its split with the East over 800 years prior. It next descended from the churches of the 16th century Reformation who protested against the doctrinal and moral faults of Rome. Finally, the Protestant Episcopal Church was an American body grown from the Church of England. This last link was its closest affinity, both chronologically and substantively, with the Episcopal Church "adopting" her English mother's "doctrine, worship, and polity, making only such changes as the differences of civil government required."[3] From the English church the Episcopalians received the Formularies: "our articles, liturgy, and homilies," which he again emphasized had undergone only small amendments from their English origins.[4]

Meade declared that these formularies defined the Episcopal Church in its doctrine, liturgy, and polity. The 39 Articles were its confession of faith with the homilies further explaining and pastorally applying such doctrine. The Prayer Book beautifully contained its rites and ceremonies with the Ordinal affirming the Formularies' commitment to episcopal government. A true churchman would concur with and adhere to these sources in what he believed, how he prayed, and how he obeyed ecclesiastical authority.

The Virginia Bishop acknowledged disagreements within the church, particularly between the "High and Low Churchman."[5] As we have discussed in this volume, these differences were real and at times intense. However, they also took place within a broader

---

[2] William Meade, "The True Churchman" (Charlottesville: James Alexander, 1851).
[3] Meade, "True Churchman," 5.
[4] *Ibid.*
[5] *Ibid.*

agreement concerning Meade's grounds for unity. Aside from some influenced by the Oxford Movement, High and Low Churchmen affirmed the Protestant, Reformational character of the Episcopal Church. Differences on questions of ceremony played out within the bounds of the Prayer Book rites and ceremonies. The factions concurred as to the goodness of Episcopal polity, even if they did not always agree on its necessity for a true church. Differences regarding ecumenicism still held both to the particulars of the Episcopal Church while acknowledging its place within a broader Church of Christ.

The Protestant Episcopal Church that Meade described had grown from a humble, even humiliating past. The Bishops described in this volume did much to make it into an important part of the American religious landscape, a church significant in numbers and even more so in theological, cultural, and political influence. Those influences began with the new American bishops. Samuel Seabury, noted Church of England bishop and historian Samuel Wilberforce—son of the antislavery crusader Willim Wilberforce—emphasized the timeliness of Seabury's arrival and its importance for the development of an American Anglican Church. Seabury "arrived at a critical time for the American Church. The first general convention was soon to meet at Philadelphia; and the knowledge that a bishop already presided over one of their Churches, greatly strengthened the hands of those who desired at once to apply for the episcopate." When the first American convention met in October 1785 in Philadelphia, "seven out of the thirteen states sent to it deputies both clerical and lay, and they entered at once on their important duties. Three leading subjects claimed their chief attention. The first of these was the general ecclesiastical constitution of the meditated union; the second, the formation of a common liturgy; the third, the steps to be taken for obtaining an American episcopate." The importance of the episcopacy to the American church was never debated. Wilberforce noted that while the development of an indigenous ecclesiastical constitution and an indigenous liturgy precipitated "warm discussion" and displayed the "various tempers" of northern and southern clergymen, they remained united on the importance of episcopal leadership. They would find that leadership in Bishop Seabury, and more importantly in Bishop William White.

Bishop White helped this church find its footing in the aftermath of the American Revolution, establishing it as a church faithful to its roots but American in its manifestation. Bishops Chase and Kemper took this church into the American wilderness, spreading the Gospel to the unreached and building up episcopal dioceses of great numbers grounded in Word and Sacrament. Bishops McIlvaine and Meade built up two powerful dioceses while contending for the authority of Scripture and the power of Gospel preaching. Bishops Hobart and Doane advocated for the importance of theological education and for guarding the distinctives of the Episcopal Church against revivalism and a too-generalizing ecumenism. And Bishop Hopkins sought bridges between factions on grounds that affirmed the Reformation and its fidelity to the Ancient Church. He, along with Doane, also sought beauty in the Church's music as well as buildings for the purpose of God receiving glory in His people's worship.

These bishops offer to Twenty-first Century Anglicans a heritage both precious and useful to our own times. To see its preciousness and its usefulness, we must first know it existed. We must first understand what it believed, how it worshiped, and in what way it was ruled. Then we might permit it to participate in forming Anglicanism in this day and age. If we do so, we will find a needed aid to our church. There is plenty of work to be done. Works on liturgy as of yet outpace works on historic Anglican political theology, particularly political theology of American Anglicans, and remains in relatively short supply. Michael Bird and N.T. Wright have published their *Jesus Among the Powers* but it is contemporaneous and oriented generally towards debates among English-speaking Evangelicals of the Twenty-First Century. There is, however, an identifiable tradition of preaching about the civil order among American Anglicans. Episcopal bishops in the Nineteenth and Twentieth Century routinely preached political sermons and wrote on political theology. Anglicans offered a necessary voice in the development of Protestant interaction with politics, but often used a different taxonomy than Evangelical Protestants in the United States. Protestant and more particularly Anglican liturgical and theological resourcement remain fruitful areas of study. Those resources show us a churchmanship grounded in the Formularies and socially, intellectual, and ecclesiastically confident in itself.

Article XIX of the 39 Articles reads, "The visible Church of Christ is a congregation of faithful men, in which the pure Word of God is preached, and the Sacraments be duly ministered according to Christ's ordinance, in all those things that of necessity are requisite to the same." Thus was the Protestant Episcopal Church. In this book, we have sought to contribute to reclaiming this heritage. We hope the stories of these bishops will inform, encourage, and, where needed, reform.

Acknowledgements

Miles Smith

My gratitude for all the help received on this project is more expansive than can be put in these acknowledgments. The origin of this book is conversations with my then rector, the Ven. Alan R. Crippen II. Archdeacon Crippen encouraged Adam and I to use our talents, meager as they are, to offer a window in to the once-glorious Protestant cultural, intellectual, and social influence provided to the American republic by Episcopal bishops in the 19th Century. Alan remains a trusted spiritual counselor and friend. He and his wife Leonor are those rare constant friends in life. For their help on this project, and their friendship, I am immeasurably grateful.

Friends at Holy Trinity Parish have assisted in various ways. Wendy and Eric Coykendall, Sam and Laura Negus, Cody and Mary Strecker, Bob Livingston, Christina Lambert, Jeremiah Regan, Isaac Waffle, Jon and Casey Gregg, and others have been available and given of their time. Our priest in charge, The Rev. John Mabus, has provided vocational and spiritual counsel regularly, and carved time out of his regular job as a navy chaplain and being a husband and father of a large family. The Rev. Adam Rick is a trusted confessor and pastor, and I am grateful for his ministry at out parish and at Hillsdale College. In our diocese the Rev. Canon Matt Kennedy, the Rev. Matt Mahan, the Rev. Jon Wylie, and the Rev. Ife Ojetayo, provide wisdom to the laity, including myself. Bishop William Love and Bishop Marc Steele are gracious fathers in God who are always available. Bishop Julian Dobbs has been a spiritual rock to me for going on a decade. I am a better man, better friend, and better husband because of him, and it is for those reasons, among others, that this work is dedicated to him.

My parents and brother, Miles, Cathy, and T. Aaron Smith, are always there for me. Adam and Emily Carrington are friends who are missed tremendously, but I am happy they are back in their beloved Ohio. Adam was one of my groomsmen when I married the person who must have the greatest acknowledgment, Jaime M. Smith. She puts up with the hours of academic life patiently and is my dearest counselor and friend. My life is immeasurably better with her influence and love. She is my daily picture of the love of Christ Jesus.

Adam Carrington

Writing a book never is a solitary endeavor. This work is not so in the obvious sense of being co-written. I am deeply grateful to Miles Smith not only for conceiving the idea for this project but for approaching me to join him in its composition. I had a special blessing in working with Dr. Smith. For, more than a co-author, I cherish Miles as a great personal friend, former colleague, and fellow churchman in the Anglican Diocese of the Living Word. Robert Ramsey at *Prolego* saw the potential of this project and guided us through its development with great patience and skill.

I also wish to thank our former rector, the Venerable Alan Crippen II, for his encouragement in bringing this book to completion. His desire to recover the history of the Protestant Episcopal Church and to retrieve that history's many virtues is contagious and an important background to this project.

Along similar lines, I wish to thank my bishop, the Rt. Rev. Julian Dobbs. He exemplifies what a bishop should be—a shepherd to the Church's shepherds, a fearless defender of the Gospel, and a tireless protector of Christ's sheep. Much of the greatness in the men profiled in this book I also see in Bishop Dobbs.

    Finally, I want to thank my wife, Emily, and our two daughters, Abigail and Eliza. To Emily, I am thankful for her steady support, wise counsel, and devotion to building Christ's Church. She has been invaluable and sacrificial in enabling this work and so much else I do to come to fruition. To my daughters, I pray you always know Jesus as your Savior, that God implants His Word deeper and deeper into your hearts, and that you know the Book of Common Prayer as it is, a masterful manner of worshipping the Lord in the beauty of holiness.

Made in the USA
Monee, IL
07 December 2025

4339ef16-d394-467d-9b9a-48be69a5abaaR01